When Comes the Call

By Lama Sing and Al Miner

Library of Congress Control Number: 2010918023

ISBN: 978-0-9828786-1-3

1. Spirit writings 2. Psychics 3. Trance Channels
I. Miner, Al II. Title

Printed in the United States of America

For books and products visit our website:
www.lamasing.net

CONTENTS

Dedication

Within the embrace of our Father's Word is the glory of knowing that one is uniquely and beautifully loved by the Father. In that knowing cometh forth a certain quality that is a treasure unto the Father and so then unto each of us.

It is unto this that we dedicate this work, as we proceed now in the light of our Father's Love.

— Lama Sing

1

Before Heaven

Imagine for a moment
that you are Consciousness,

and that you have only
this one awareness ...

that you are at peace,

... and that you are.

As the light begins to appear,
we become aware of our uniqueness.

We look upon one another with a gladness
and a sense of brilliance all about.

We look beyond, after a time,
and we see the unfolding and dancing
between the various energies and forces.

Then, upon a time, we gather again here and there, exploring one another and the awareness that each holds in their beauty and uniqueness.

Several gather and decide to go forth in a certain way, to follow these energies as they are moving, and we join them. As we do, the interaction of their consciousness with the energies begins to manifest something heretofore not understood.

But we can move into this.

As each interaction manifests, we become it ... to experience it, and to know it.

Then, we move into oneness ... and separate, in order that we shall know one another in the completeness of each of these experiences.

Each experience is ours.

So it continues, and the light expands and interacts beautifully, with such wonder. The realms of consciousness, the realms of question, inquisitiveness, begin to move in divergent ways.

Upon the movement of these divergencies, there comes about the consciousness of those who seek, now greater and greater, to create. As they so do, they discover that they are capable of creation in such a manner that delights them.

So we come to them, as in the past, to share with them.

But they have moved away, into their creations. We honor their choices and we observe.

Many others move off to explore and experience in ever-expanding and unique ways.

We ponder with joy the presence of that Spirit, that Form, that Force of Creation, which we know is our Source. After a time, we move back into our Source, and find the joy of Its completeness yet as it was in the first moments.

And we celebrate with our new consciousness.

After a time, we decide (and discuss with our Father) and journey forth seeking our brethren to celebrate with them. These are not idle activities, but of majesty that is beyond description. These are those creative forces that are ever in motion throughout eternity, and we are one with them!

We turn about to observe our Father and give to Him our love, and we see that in return. We know that He wishes us to be free to explore and journey.

So we do, with greater and greater joy, tasting the sweet wine of freedom.

After a time, we encounter others of our brethren here

and there, and we celebrate with them, with ease and joy, the beauty of their creations. We understand from them that they have shaped the various forces of creation of the Word of God into that which is of wondrous beauty, such as we have not known separate from us ... always within us.

We move into these creations with ease, and feel them, and see the source of these creations within us as that which is our Father within.

Then, we come back to our uniqueness, and we celebrate the beauty as each one has partaken of it.

We encounter another grouping of our brethren who have created a form, that which they now dwell in. We look upon them with laughter and joy, and we learn so much from their creations. And we realize that this and greater lies within ... that, indeed, our Father continues to give to us the same as in the first moment, whereupon He sent the Word forth, and the light came.

We look at the wellspring of God's love within, and we reach within, into that well of God's love and beauty, and we bring it forth in this way and that. We see the beauty of God as we bring it into this form or that. We see that which is called Color, and we begin to hear the sound of our own laughter in a new way, that resonates within form, that vibrates in such a way that the beautiful shades and color give us their song of wonder, the energy of their expression of the Source ... of God.

We move about in wondrous ways and we create as we do, and we find this brings even more beautiful energies as we interact with one another. As each gives unto that intention another form is created; and in that form is the uniqueness of each of us. We will the form to move and to dance upon the colors and the sounds, and give unto us a mirror of our own being. We taste of it. We feel it. We hear it. We see it. And we do so for the first time from the form of definition.

We move instantly with ease into the infinite, where we are one with the All ... we move ... and move ...

And we feel a curious reaction in the All. We look upon one another, and we ask of other groupings, "Do you know of this?"

They tell us they know of it, but they know not what it is ... perhaps some new work on the part of some of our brethren. But they do not wish to seek it. Their joy is in their presence in God, in these creations and the greater as they continually call them forth from within.

We move, now, beyond that which is, into that which is not.

As we continue to move in our oneness with God and in the perfect harmony of God's creation, others of our brethren come forth from within the All, and the beauty of their presence resonates all throughout us.

As they look upon us, they ask with love in their words and spirits, "What have you created ... and why?"

We give to them that which we are, and thus they know.

Then they answer our question. "There are those of the Children who have gone forth beyond the manifestation of God and into their own creations, just as we see that you have experienced and tasted and known."

We ask them, "Why do you not journey so as our brothers there in the light, dancing and singing, making these manners so as to send their joy unto God, building creations that God can know these as His Children's good works, and moving with His Will, His Spirit, as it goes forth knowing Itself and knowing us through our creations and our beauty? These we see as good things. Why do you not come and partake of them with us?"

They answer in this manner: "We have seen these, but we have chosen not to participate nor be one with them; for as we began to approach them, we could feel, we knew, that these things might, indeed, in a manner, separate us from our beloved Father and from our oneness with all and He. We love this, the All, within which we can know God as in the beginning and as in the ending and all in between.

"But we celebrate you, dear friends. We see the gladness within you and because you know it, of course we know it; but we choose, you see, to remain here in the embrace of God, which, as you can see, envelops all and greater that you have given to us of your knowledge.

"Those whom you seek are there ... where the All interacts with the creations. They are moving into their creations in ways that are *defining* ... something impossible to conceive of! Thus, as they create this impossibility, because they are the Children of God, they are manifesting it as though it were real, as though it could possibly be. And here, you see, in the All at the edge of creation, they do so believing that it will not be known. For they have moved so deep into their creations that it is increasingly difficult for them to regain their true nature."

We question our brothers in the All, understanding immediately because they give it to us.

Then we journey to see these of our brethren who believe themselves to be *separate*, to be in such a manner that we cannot conceive of even though we have journeyed within the creations.

We pass through the creations of the Children of God, and the pure originating Will of God, moving, yet moving. We marvel at the contrast side-by-side ... the pure delight of God beginning to express in ways that are of such wondrous definition and contrast. We sweep into God's Will, the Force, and joyfully allow ourselves to soar upon the varying tones and qualities of His Will moving ... freely, wondrously, joy abounding.

We become one with He. We become one.

Yet we are that we are.

Some of our grouping move off to explore a singular expression. Like a thread among a fabric of gold, it has a hint of uniqueness. They return to tell us of it, and they give to us that which is their experience. We know it, and thus we are one again. The journey of each of these, while separate, you see, empowers us to be one with them because they choose it, and return in their completeness that they would know that they are always one with us and we with them. In that manner we are never separate, and yet always we are unique.

So we journey, realizing our uniqueness. Somehow the creative waves and colors, sounds, and the glory of God seems to emphasize the unique beauty of each, and we pause to celebrate it as it manifests more and more completely. We move from one to the other, and to another, and to another, until all here have been seen and known for their beauty as God obviously intends it.

Knowing our uniqueness, when we once again come together, our oneness begins to create in a manner we have not known. Something wonderful occurs. We can see the Will, the Force, of God, moving from within each of us to come into oneness, and then move forth from us as though we are God expressing these majestic, wondrous creative forces moving out into the existence of the Will of God!

Here, we see the reflections of each of us, and we move wondrously, weaving in and out, pausing to bathe ourselves in the uniqueness of these dizzying arrays of wondrous glory. Each of us lets the other be them, that we might know them.

Then we move into groupings, that the others can know the uniqueness of our grouping as a singular expression of harmony, of beauty ... a symphony of the wonders of God.

We come together and we pause for a moment.
We focus again upon our Father, and ask of Him.
He tells us,
This is who and what you are. You are so beautiful. Create after yourselves, as I create you, and let the glory of our oneness find new expression, new manifestation into that which you know not in the present.

We realize that what we have seen and experienced is only the beginning.

Then one in our grouping remembers, and asks, "What of our brethren who have gone to That-Place-That-Does-Not-Exist?"

We look upon him and we see within him something curious. We all come to feel it, to know it; we move to him and we become him, and we see and we begin to feel as he feels.

Then we move apart, and we discuss this. "What is this? It is not clearly of our knowledge."

He who has asked that thing remembers God clearly. As he does, he becomes illuminated with His presence and His oneness, and we see then that he has found a pathway to our brethren who are in that Place. We take his knowing, together, and we become one with it.

So we follow his knowing to where they are, and we begin to encounter something quite odd ... curious. At first, it seems that it cannot be so. As we continue to journey it becomes moreso and moreso predominant.

We pause to look at one another and to be each other, and we all feel it and sense it.

He speaks again, our brother, "Let us move away from this for a time."

So we do.

We go within, in oneness, and we become a light unto ourselves and we become one with our Father. We return to our uniqueness, as we have journeyed within to our Father.

He assures us,

All is well. What you have tasted is the uniqueness of expression that is of their choosing.

They wish to know definition in a different way. So, remember me and claim my presence within you, and move with ease and joy. And as you come upon that which is unknown to you, know it; and I will know it with you. I am one with you always. As you remember this, as you have done, we shall find the gladness in our journeys. Shall we not?

As we reawaken our uniqueness, and create our unique light and oneness simultaneously, we turn, as he, our brother, calls upon us again, "Let us journey to look upon them, and see what works they do."

So we move, again, with our oneness with our Father reaffirmed in our presence.

We come upon others who have come to this Place and paused, as we did earlier, and we find them in a place of rest. We go to them and we invite them to let us be one with them, and so we do; and we celebrate and rejoice, and we know them and let them know us.

We discover that the uniqueness of this Place has defined itself to be limited ... wherein certain qualities and essences are the predominant. These predominant essences have called upon something of God to make it so, and so it is! So we reach into this Place and know it, and we see that those who have gone before us have placed this here, that they can be as they wish. We celebrate their decision; and we know this Place, and we look upon one another and become each other, that we can know it from the uniqueness of one another.

We become one. We move to the Father, and we celebrate with our Father and He with us.
He tells us,
Be of good joy. These Children have begun to create after a fashion that they have discovered within them.

He reminds us that we are all one.

We journey back to our oneness, and then call to our own uniqueness, and claim this again. We move about, to know this Place completely. We see it as a broad curving elemental of the creation of God that has been defined by intention. The elementals here do not wish the other elementals to be one with it; they wish to be unique unto themselves as a part of, and yet uniquely separate from, the Creative Force.

Our brother calls upon us, and we agree, and we move within. We decide, then, that we shall journey further and see what works they have done beyond this.

With the thought of our Father embracing us and we embracing He, we move with ease.

We realize that we are in yet a different element very soon. We taste it and know it, and take it within.

Some in our grouping decide that their choice is not to be one with this element; that they feel something that does not bring them the completeness of the joy that they have always known. They call for oneness. So, as we become one, we embrace each other. We know them, and we invite them to know us, and we detect, then, instantly that these elements have had an impact upon these brethren.

We decide to move away from this Place and beyond the first element into the All once again.

To our joy, our brethren of the All are here to embrace us, and we instantly become one. They move all throughout us and throughout those who have tasted of the second element and found it not in harmony completely. Our brethren of the All purify them, and they take this memory and transform it into just that ... a definition.

We move within and become one, and return to our Father. We speak to Him of this.

As He assures us that He knows it, He also tells us again,

Those of you who have known this second element, and find it not to be in harmony with your completeness, then do as you are ... and respond to what you feel, and do not dwell in that second element.

This little grouping then looks to our Father with their completeness, and asks of Him, "Why, sweet Father, would this second element, created by our brethren, not wish to harmonize with us? Why is it that we react and have this feeling, when these of our other brothers who have journeyed to the second element with us are at peace in it?"

He embraces them all, and He speaks to them softly,

Sweet Children, now you know one of the greatest gifts I have given you ... You are beginning to see how unique you are. And because this second element took away a tiny portion of your joy, then know that it is not for you.

It is not that it is to be judged by you in any way, but only, dear Children, that you know it in its uniqueness. And you look within yourselves and come to me, as you have; and we will look upon it together, and know it. You can decide that your joy is elsewhere than in the second element. But that should in nowise have impact upon you to create what you have created.

"And what is that, sweet Father?" they ask together.

You have created separateness. You have created that within yourself this is not a part of you. And yet it is within me, and thus it is within you.

Know this, then: You have my gift of Choice. If you find that this second element does not speak to you in a manner that gladdens you from within ...

He touches each of them where He is ever within them.

Then, do as that which harmonizes you. Be, within and about, that which brings you the completeness of the joy that you have known previously and shall know forever.

And know this: Deny nothing; but choose that as brings you the completeness of your joy. What you have

23

created, in this experience, is now in my creation. When you encounter such again, remember my words, and remember where I have touched you, that you can go there and find the understanding of these words ever with you.

As we move back to our uniqueness and as we are together in oneness, we know something that we have never known before.

This little grouping of our brothers and sisters, those who have the uniqueness of these creations, have decided to move away from this Place.

Something within us, all of us, is reacting to their *choice*, as our Father calls it. So we decide to move with them.

We move back from the All into creation, and we continue our journey.

As we are moving within and without the collage of wondrous creative essences of God in their pure form, we pause, and our brother speaks again. "I wish to know our brethren who have gone into this Place. Who will journey with me?"

Immediately we feel that which we have known a time ago.

We come into oneness and we ask of our Father, "Father, what is this feeling, when we consider leaving these of our brethren who find in the second element that which makes them feel incomplete? How can we leave them? Can we keep on knowing our oneness with them, if we go back to the second element?"

Our Father smiles, and answers,

Yes. You can always keep this oneness with them.
Know this: As you have come together and sought me, so in that same manner can you come together and

know them. You speak of this second element as though it is apart from me and apart from your brethren. It is a creation of those of your brethren who are intending it. But it is not separate. They define it in that manner, but all is one.

But all is honored, you see; lest all of the beauty you have experienced with such joy would not be expressed in its glorious uniqueness.

What you have just created and called in this manner is the uniqueness. And the movement from the proximity of oneness into the uniqueness of one another gives you the capability to understand through the seeing. But you know, as you have done so, that as you will it, you can move into oneness, and there, we shall be together.

One of our brethren asks, "Lord, how can we know this when there is this feeling? Something within seems to be different. I hear Your words, and I hear and I feel Your presence. What is this thing? I wish it not to be within me. Can You take it from me?"

We all turn with wonder to look upon this one, and then look upon our Father. Suddenly we realize something … This one has created something we have known not.

Our Father gives us that opportunity to ponder this.

Then He answers that one,

Let us call what you have brought forth from within you … a new thing … let us call this fear. When you move into such a thought, you forget that you and I are always one. Didn't you?

The one who is asking marvels at this, and the uniqueness of his being begins creating and manifesting … here, right in our oneness with God!

We are in wonder of it.

"Oh, Father!" he calls out, "Take this thing from me. I

do not wish it to be. If I have created it, would that Thou would take it from creation!"

The Father smiles, and says unto him,

If I create a thing, sweet son, would you adjudge it to be good, or bad?

Instantly, that one responds to God, "Oh, no! Within You is such a wonder, a peace, an essence which is only good."

Then, you are of me, my Child. If you believe that this thing that you see within you is not of me, then we should, indeed, take it from you. But if you see that you and I are one, then surely we must together have found this thing. And it simply is.

What you have within you is the realization of what your brethren, my Children, have begun the creation of. In the expression of the uniqueness of the second element, they are intensifying their separateness, their individuality. They are simply creating a manifestation of their uniqueness to such a degree that it seems utterly separate. But it is, indeed, always one.

Know this, then, all of you, and He embraces dearly this one who has asked: *Because you discover these new elements, these new choices on the part of one another, and you find that within you something is not as complete when you are in those creations, then do not believe that I am not present, but recognize that you are not in harmony with it; that it is not the second element that is bad or wrong or in discord with I, but it is your reaction to it, only because you know it not.*

We celebrate, and bring joy to our Father, and He returns it to us, as always, so many times over.

We take this and give it to one another, and we embrace our brother who has asked, and he is complete again. He takes this thing within him that he has asked the

Father of and he holds it up that we might all see it and know it, and so we do. We realize, now, that it is only an intention; that it is the intent, the thought of our brethren, creating. We marvel at the consistency of it and the uniqueness of its separateness.

We embrace our Father, and we return to our oneness and into our forms of uniqueness, once again.

Those with our brother who have looked upon the second element and known it, now choose not to be a part of that or the journey beyond. They will remain here in the presence of the brethren of the All, and they will be with us as our Father has said.

We pause before the first and second element, and we embrace each other; and we form a great envelopment around the first and second element ... so great, that we come unto ourselves once again, beyond it. As we have done this we realize, with wonder and awe, that we have completely enveloped the first and second element.

We pause in our oneness as we envelop the first and second element.

We hear our Father's light laughter.

Suddenly, we know ... We, together, in our intention, have created in a manner not unlike those who have created the first and second element, and because we have decided that this is not a part of the first and second element, we realize with great mirth and humor, in the process of our *be*-ing, we have, inadvertently, created the third element.

Our intention was and is that it is ever one with God, and not separate. Thus, we have embraced that which defines itself in its uniqueness, and in the creation of our love and our embrace, and our oneness with the Father, so does it now exist.

We decide to call this the Heaven Place.

2

Knowing Separateness

Following the path of our brother's realization, as he had prepared it, we move through our third element, and through the first and second elements, with such an ease that we embrace one another with joy for the delight of it. We engage that within, and see the beauty and vastness of it, and so we soar upon that which clearly holds the uniqueness of these, our brethren who had claimed their uniqueness.

Some in our grouping note very swiftly that some beloved energies, creations, are not present. We know these for their unique expression of freedom and wondrous spontaneous creativity. Yet all about, here, there seems to be a prevailing sense of definition.

We continue to move within.

While these are not defined, we see them, and we know them, and move into them, just as though they might be, perhaps, the beginning formulation of yet another element. Curious ... We know these energies quite well, and we see the role that they have played elsewhere in creation. But, here, we find the curious energies, as though someone has placed a constraint upon them, and we can feel and sense the wonders that are within those constraints.

We pause to look at one another and embrace, to feel ... that we each know this unique beauty, and we ask him, "Do you know what keeps it? Why is it not free?"

Softly, with an understanding that we reach out to embrace, he tells us it is because they have set it to be so.

Some in our grouping ask, "Why? Why would anyone take this beauty and constrain it?"

We come together with them, to embrace them, and, though some passage of a curious feeling transpires, it comes to be: It seems as though our embrace and our sharing are also constrained.

But he calls us forth, and embraces us, and reminds us that we are the Father's Children, that He is with us.

We celebrate this and we become one. Soon all is well, and we are filled with joy of our oneness.

We move forward from this sweet little color, little sound, little energy. Even though we love it so, we trust in our brethren and their decision, and we move forward within in that trust.

Soon, we encounter yet another familiar creative Force of God. They have shaped this curiously.

We move into this shape, and we know it. We move to the boundaries of it.

So many in our group respond in such a way that the decision is made that we shall leave this Place.

We become one, and move, and come before our Father. And we joyfully embrace Him. As He touches each of us, we feel His sweet caress.

Gently, He asks of us,

What thing do you share in, and bring here to me?

One comes forth and, radiant with his love of his Father, answers, "O, Father, we journeyed, and followed him," pointing to he who has led us.

Our Father looks upon him and smiles.

And what did you find upon this journey, dear Child?

"We found You, O Father. But ... They have bound You up! The first was likened unto the other ... two elements. They were, indeed, pure. Yet, their life, their beauty, was contained, so much so, that, rather than to lift us up ... Oh-h, Father, I cannot say it."

The others come to this one and embrace him.

Our Father smiles.

After a time, allowing us to feel ... all of us to feel this one's experience ... we hear Him say, *You have come to know another thing. Is it true?*

We answer in unison, "It is ... and not one, but another, and we believe other such of Your beautiful gifts to us have been curiously bound, Father. Why? Why are they kept from expression?"

After a time, the Father brings one of them to be with us. After embracing him, the Father sets him before us and asks, *Good Child, these are thy brethren. Do you know them?*

He turns about quickly, this way and that.

At first, we do not know him, for he cannot see us as we are.

Then, the Father touches him, and after a time, we can see him see us. We rush to him.

But the Father intercedes, *Give your brother a moment. He has been on a great journey.*

We step back in wonder and awe at this one of our brothers, who has actually been deep within that Place-That-Is-Not. We see our Father communing with our brother, but we turn to one another in wonder! "Why do we not hear them? Why do we not know what it is?"

We feel something so distantly odd some in our grouping do not wish to remain here. They depart.

We see them soaring off into Consciousness, and we long for them, for we love them dearly. But we honor our Father, and so we do as we know He wishes us to do. But we cannot build that awareness that knows this experience.

Then our Father touches us again, and we feel His love.

Quickly, one among us speaks, "Father ... look!" He points off into Consciousness, "Why did they leave?"

Gently, the Father responds to us,
They do not wish this experience. They have
chosen, dear Children. And that is their right.

"But, Father! Are we not one?"

Smiling, the Father turns to the one who has
come from within No-Where, and then back to us.
Indeed, we are one. But you are growing, and
learning, and you are creating. You are discovering
wondrous things. And you will come unto those places
and things that will know you not; even though you, in
your oneness can reach out and know them, they will
not say to you, "Welcome, let me know you. Come
and know me."

Several in our grouping begin to generate strange
energies and colors.

Our Father intercedes, and nods to us not to intercede
with their experience.

The Father touches them, and sayeth unto
them,
Come closer. All of you ... Come. Let us be one, and
let me show you ...

Those who have left our grouping are journeying with
great rapidity through Consciousness.

Some of our brethren from other groupings see them,
and come to instantly be with them. "What journey are you
upon, good brothers and sisters?"

When there is no immediate response, they
immediately become one with our separate brothers and
sisters, and then they know. They all pause, that they can
become one, and in their oneness they balance with this
thing, which is not known.

One within the grouping calls out, "Let us move into

oneness with our Father, and ask Him, 'What is this thing?'"

Even those who had left the experience and the other members of their grouping are now at peace through the Oneness.

Swiftly, in a twinkling, they are present.

The Father reaches out to them, and embraces them, and they become one. And we embrace them, with our Father, and joy and peace abound. We revel in our oneness and we celebrate with our Father. Our love, shared and exchanged, becomes a thing of beauty. Spires of wonder go forth, rolling with ease and sweetness off into Consciousness, and we know that others of our grouping will see this and feel it, and as they do they will come.

So they do. More and more of the groupings come, and we are one, and as we become one, our joy expands, and the Father's love becomes more brilliant.

We look about, and there are others coming, answering the Father's call of love ... leaving the Place of No-Where!

We look upon them, and we feel a momentary feeling, and the Father touches us and we feel only love and joy.

The Father embraces them, and we as well, and we are all one.

Then, one asks of our Father, "Father, what of the beauty of Your creation as Your Word has gone forth? Is it no more because we are all one again?"

We see our Father smile upon him,
Precious son, do you wish it to be?
Turning to all of us, He asks the same.

Without a pause, "Yes, Father! We love the beauty of You expressed in these unique, wondrous ways. And Father, when we come unto them and we bring them together, we see You creating even greater, more and more, and we feel You within us. We touch these things and they respond, as though to ask us, 'What would you have us do?

What would you have us be?' We have but to tell them,
Father, and they do that thing for us! Oh, Father ... These
are great and glorious gifts You have given us. Yes, we
would wish them to be."
> *Very well.*
> The Father states this quietly, with love and a
> bit of laughter as a hint within Him, though all of
> us feel it.

So we move into the joy of our oneness, and we
celebrate creation. We laugh together, and sing and dance,
and we hold the light of our Father's glory up as we have all
experienced it and gathered it, that our Father can see it as
we do and know it as we have known it.
> He smiles and nods to us,
> *So is it then.*

We rush to be embraced by Him, and we embrace one
another as well.
> Our Father says unto us,
> *Children, I have another gift for you, and so let me
> bring it forth ...*
> *That which you have known and has always been,
> shall ever be, and I shall place it here. And intertwining
> with the edge of it I shall place my Word, that the
> creation, which you love and which brings you such joy,
> can be forever attached to the embrace of this ... the All,
> that always has been and ever shall be.*

The joy of the Children of the All flows with wondrous
abundance and celebration, and we laugh with them and
delight with them. For all here know and love the All, for it
is the house of our Father, and our house.
> *And look you here,* the Father sayeth unto us.
> *Look you upon this, and know it ...*

In a moment's passing, we see a beautiful striated form
go forth upon the Word of our Father, and cascading here

and there we see it being taken into all of creation.

The Father tells us,

This is a good thing that I have placed before you: It can give you understanding. So, go forth and celebrate. I am with you.

Some go immediately.

Others hesitate, turning back to embrace the Father again and again. He touches them and gives them the goodness of their own being, calling it to the forefront. So they, too, move forward.

The Father looks upon those who have gone into the All. He gives to them the awakening of that which has gone forth into the Word, and He tells them,

This is good. Find joy in this as your brethren shall find joy in it, in their own ways, according to their choices.

In our grouping now are some of those who came from that Place-Which-Cannot-Be, but now we begin to understand what they intend. As they say unto us that they wish to return to that Place and continue their works therein, we become one with them that they will know, ever, that we are one.

They tell us, "Join us as you will. We welcome you."

We follow them, and we come to the edge of our Father's Word and the All, as He has called it. We delight in moving through the dance of the Light and the Darkness of the All. We celebrate the glory of this.

We turn to show our love to the Father.

We hear His gentle laughter and we know it is good.

We look to one another and we dance, and we laugh and celebrate, and we feel and hear the Forces that are in the All call to us, embracing us, as we have always been. The beauty and wonder of it sweeps all throughout that which we know, and we hurtle ourselves into the All, spinning about, dancing, calling out with our color and sound. The Children of the All come to be with us, and we become one with them.

Then comes One who is of the Children of the All, who has come to shine brightly with His love of God so much so that it is nigh unto looking upon God. We find this of great joy, and so, of course, we much embrace Him. After a moment's embrace, we all step back, that we can see His uniqueness.

He sayeth unto us, *"Come, and look upon this. It has come from our Father's Word, to touch the edge of the All."*

As we come to look upon it, we see our Heaven in its beauty and love and compassion, which was our intent as we gave it! We are in wonder and joy, that it is yet present.

He-Who-Shines-In-The-All comes to us and tells us, *"The Father sayeth that, that which you believe and hold within you, is. The love and compassion that you have felt for your brethren within that No-Where will be here, the Father says, forever.*

We ask He-Who-Shines-In-The-All, "What is this ... *Forever?"*

He laughs so much that we must laugh with Him, and that which we are as unique comes forth and dances with the other uniquenesses, and we become one swiftly and then swiftly return to our individuality.

He tells us, with a smile as our Father, *"Remember when you went to embrace that Nowhere-Place, and you came upon yourselves, and realized that you had fully embraced it?*

"It is like that ... Eternity, we now know, is that place where you come upon yourself and you celebrate, and you become the

greater. And then a new journey, new wonders, follow. But I know them not, for, as yet, only the Father knoweth these. And He said, Seek it. It is there for you, *and we know it to be good, because the Father has given it.*"

We marvel how our Heaven element shines in the great sea of the All.

"Beautiful, is it not?" He says unto us.

"Indeed. But what is within?"

We pause to become one.

We ask of our Father, "What is now within our Heaven Place, Father ... that element we've created without the knowledge of its creation?"

The Father gently answers,

How do you know what is within a brother or a sister?

One answers, with joy, "I simply go to them, and I know them. We become one, and we know you."

With a twinkle, the Father answers,

Then Children, why not the same for this, which you call No-Where, No-Place, and other such titles?

I tell you, if you turn now and look upon it, you will see that it is. And now you have the gift of understanding, if you seek it and use it.

If you wish to know what is within, then know it. If you do not, then so shall it be.

Our grouping moves with joy and excitement. We contemplate knowing this Nowhere-Place-That-Is (because the Father sayeth it, thus it is) and we come upon it, and we pause.

We look about and we see some of our brethren gift to us their uniqueness, and tell us they are with us but choose not to go within. Rather, they wish to continue their journey, and *be.*

Some who are Children of the All embrace us and tell us that they are ever near at hand. If we would but have a need to ask of them, they shall give it in His Name.

Oh-h, the joy and excitement! We shall know this thing! Perhaps some of our brethren are there, waiting for us to celebrate.

We can come into oneness within this great element of Heaven. We move into the element that is ours of creation, and we rejoice. It bathes us. It is as though some aspect of our Father is alive here. We move through this, and we use something curious that we have found ... We can look this way and that way, and this way and that way, and it seems to define itself to us. So now we turn to look in the way which is to go within, and we come upon the first element. Because we know it, it accepts us and we pass through with ease. We feel the difference. It creates something within us ... an energy that is secondary. Each of us describes it differently.

We move into one, and then another, and then another, that we can know this thing. So we do, and we bring peace to it, and give peace as our gift to this thing. And we move deeper ... deeper. We look back, and here and there, we can see this thing, which the Father tells us is definition. We move in the definition until we come to the beginning of the second element, and we move more slowly now in honor of those of our brethren who experience this with that thing the Father told them they had created. But we have no sense of it other than to know it is here if we wish to be one with it. We do not, so we simply continue.

Now we move further in the direction within this Place, and we find that one of the earlier experiences has now become an element. It clearly has dimension. It has conformity, and something that brings it into a unique state of oneness with itself but not the other elements.

We move more, noting this, and we come to yet the

next substance or thing and see that it is already forming yet another element, and because it is not completely formed, we pass through curious little ... we call them *pieces* of the thing that will become an element. They are very smooth, and we touch them as we pass by, and we feel their uniqueness. The next and the next are all the same.

We look towards that pathway from whence we come, and we see that they are becoming one. We smile upon this and find joy in it, because it is so like our oneness. And we journey through more of these, less and less dense.

We ponder, "What could our brethren be creating?"

After just a bit of this contemplation, we come unto the great opening. Swiftly, there is this feeling of the Father's peace. Yet, as we look about, we see that the elements are wrapped all around this peace!

And we begin to feel a longing for the Father.

He comes to gather us all about, and we join Him. We become one.

> The Father speaks to us softly,
> *Be of good cheer. I am ever with you. Be free.*

So we joyfully move into our uniqueness, and we continue on.

Then we begin to see some of our brethren. They are very active. They are moving about here and there, and some ... Curious, as we watch them from one of these distances away. They collide with one another, but they do not become one! "What have they done to themselves?"

So we rush up to the one who has bounced off the other, and we say to him, "Our greetings. What is it that you do?"

There is a curious emptiness, and we hear him, "I am about my works."

"And what are they?" we ask. "Shall we become one,

and do them together?"

After a time, we hear, "I am about my works. Perhaps we can do that later," and he is gone!

"What is this curious thing of our brethren?"

We go to another, and we experience much the same, and another, and another.

We pause to look about. So many of our brethren are so active … moving here, there … gathering up the energies, and …

"What do they do with them?"

"They are taking them within?"

"Why do they not set them free?"

Some in our grouping begin to vibrate in a curious way, so we turn to them and ask, "Are you creating? Like these, our brethren?"

At first, they do not answer, but then we hear within, "No. We have become one because we do not wish this to be a part of us."

"How can this be?" we ask. "Are we not all one?"

Then, with a light's appearance, a brilliance, they become unique before us.

One comes forward and states, "They do not wish to be one with us. Why would we dwell here in this No-Place with these of our brethren who have befallen this strange … *separateness?* It is something that befalls them when they come into this Place. It is like a strange energy that afflicts those who enter in here." They become one again. The solidity of their oneness is remarkable, and we hear them speak as one, "We do not wish to dwell in this Place. It does not hold the peace of our Father and His joy."

He, the brother, comes forward and speaks to them, "Look you, look within. You know this cannot be. Our Father has said it … Wherever we are, He is there. Whatever we wish, He will answer it. Let us become one, and ask of our Father."

They do not answer. Then, they say, "Yes, sweet brother. We know you and we know your love. Let us not become one here, lest their energy becomes one with us and we become like they ... separate. Let us leave this Place, and become one beyond it. We are leaving, now!"

We watch with wonder, as the beauty of their oneness begins to move back along the pathway upon which we entered.

So he, the brother, sayeth to us, "Let us become one and follow. They need our love."

So we follow them.

We see the beauty of their light just ahead of us on this path, and we see ... very strange ... These elements, that were forming behind us, have now formed, and we see our brethren in their oneness, moving this way and that upon the innermost element.

"What do they do?" we ask our brother.

"Let us go to them, and be one with them. They have lost the way."

Immediately, we become one with them, and we embrace them. We place them within the center of our being.

We hear our brother say, "Look you, here. Here is our oneness, and here is the Father. Father, give to us your light that it will show us the way from This-Place-That-Is-Not."

Immediately, we see the path open before us, shining, and we feel our Father's love.

We move swiftly, easily, and we look out to see here is one such element ... and now another, and another, and another. We become so thankful that we have our oneness with our Father. This Place surely must be created of He, but they do not respond to us ... They know us not!

We hear the Father speak gently,

No ... What you are contemplating is not so. It is merely the choices of your brethren, whom you have seen, about their various works. That is all. Nothing more. It is not separate of I nor you ... only your sensitivity to it. See?

You know it not, in the sense of being one with it. So therefore, it is not one with you. When you know a thing, then it has a place within you. When you know it not, it is as this ... You choose it to be outside of self.

We rush to our Father to embrace Him and He to embrace us. As He touches us, each one, we feel something different. We feel that He has touched us in a way that we now see as clearly evident upon each of us, and we turn to look at one another.

One in our grouping sayeth, "See? It is as I have said it! Those elements, that Place has placed its energy within us. Look you upon me! Look you, here, upon my brother! See it?"

Again, we see the strangeness of the energies and beautiful raiment that shine forth from him.

Our Father's gentleness touches him and embraces him.

Call forth, sweet Child, that which has been and know it, and in the knowing all will be well. The illusion of that which is not known seeks to sustain itself according to the will of those who give it life, but the life with you is me and we, together, are the All.

We turn to journey into the All, and we feel the joy of this place where we are. We look about ... beyond ... beyond that Place, where the Father's Word and light dance upon the edge of this which has always been.

And we know this beautiful Darkness to be our Home.

3

Definition

The journeys continue long and far. We journey off to visit with other brethren. We come into oneness and allow to flow the creative potential that is our combined force given us by God to flow. As this flows from us we move further along that which we have chosen, and in our movement we encounter other brethren who see this and know it to be good. So they come unto us. We celebrate them and, together, we journey along this intent.

We feel the sweetness and simplicity and the wonder of being embraced by the thought of God.

"We feel You with us, Father, and we are joyful."

We perceive others of our brethren here and there moving about through the beauty of the Word of God, and we come unto them again, and again, and each time, we find the joy of our oneness to bring to us such a glory, such a wonder.

We contemplate what we have experienced as Father has asked us to go forth, and we contemplate His gifts to us and we share these.

Then, our grouping turns and wheels off into the beauty of the unfolding echo of the sound and color of the Word of God moving and touching, and bringing light and joy and color.

Here, we find brethren celebrating the colors and the sounds and the beautiful essences ... *energies*, they will be called, and we know this.

We soar along this particular energy, this part of the Word of God, as it seems to call unto us. We move and soar together in oneness, and then we move apart and celebrate this from each entity's perspective. Each of our brothers and sisters see this and know its goodness.

Upon a time, we pause, and we come together and share with one another.

We look about at ourselves and our brethren and see the beauty that is ours. As we see this, we know the Father in each of our brethren! It causes us to come to them and ask to be one with them. We begin to laugh as we become one, together, in this grouping and that, and then over here in the beauty of these energies, and then up above, and below, as these have come into definition by the brothers and sisters in the No-Place.

When we contemplate them, a strange occurrence comes about our grouping, and we pause to look at this, to taste of it, to feel it, to know it, to take it into our being.

Then we know. We become one, and in our oneness there is great peace and ease ... such a wonderful resonance as we are one.

Then the Father cometh.

We ask of Him, "Father, what is this thing? We have looked at it, we have moved it all about. But it is not as we have seen in our joyful experiences."

The Father listens quietly and smiles, nodding.

It is that part of you, dear Children, that calls to you as you seek to be one.

Then he, our brother, comes forward and asks of the Father, "Why do they not come as we call to oneness? Why do they not answer our call?"

The Father looks upon him and embraces him, that he might know completely His love for him. Then, He turns and looks upon us all and embraces us all together, and we feel the goodness again.

The brother and several of our brethren come before God again and ask, "Father, have *we* created this thing?"

The Father smiles upon them so sweetly,

My Children, do not think that you are the cause of what you feel. There is that which goes into our creation, which brings forth the opportunity of

45

definition. Such a definition, that you can build
understanding ... as I have told you.

He and the brothers ask, "Father, why do you give us
this thing? It does not feel of the joy and wonder that we
know is Your gift to us that we know is You."

Again, He embraces us and whispers to us
sweetly,
Be of good cheer and good peace.
Know this: I am ever with thee, and all things are
of me. If in a moment, such as you discovered in
knowing the thing, you feel a separateness, you have the
power to bring me to that Place, that thing. And then
my presence within it will be known.

He releases us to look upon us, everyone,
touching some here and there.

Then he and the brethren come forth again, "Father,
where are our brethren who do not answer our call? Do
they yet dwell in the No-Place?"

The Father smiles upon them, beautifully.
Perhaps it is so, my Children. And is this something
which brings to you this thing?

The brother turns to commune with his brothers and
sisters, and they agree to answer our Father. "The *thing* is
their absence, Father. It is something we have not known
other than the experiences as we encountered the elements,
but we know You are there. But yet, this thing ..."

There is silence among all the children, for
immediately, all feel the presence of the thing.

Then the Father calls us all to Him and embraces us
again.

He sayeth unto us,
Know this: Feel my embrace. It is within you. It is
you. Only that which seems separate can be separate.
Do you understand?

He releases us, to look upon us.

Our brother and the brethren answer, "We understand what you have given, Father, clearly, as always. Then this *thing* is their absence. Are we not ever one with them?"

The Father comes very, very close to he and our brethren.

Are we one?

They rush to the Father and answer, "We are one, Father. We love You."

Then what are you creating, sweet Children?

Moving away, the Father looks upon them with a loving smile.

"Oh Father, we do not do this thing. It happened! And as You said, it is not ours ... we are encountering it. It is, as You have said, something that wishes to be unto itself. Is this what You have called definition?"

It is definition. And it is the reaction, see ... the result of your brethren who are doing works they consider to be good in that No-Place, as you have lovingly called it.

He and the brethren look at one another and begin to laugh. "Oh Father, we must tell you that our first thoughts, our first feelings, our first experiences were not that of love."

The Father is smiling very broadly. Softly, in a whispering voice,

Are you saying, sweet Children, that you had a time wherein you did not know love?

They look at one another with swiftness, and something even different, and they become very excited in their uniqueness.

The Father laughs softly,

I see you are understanding.

After a brief time, they become calm and peaceful, and they have returned to oneness. Then, they speak to the Father, "Have we done this thing, Father? Is it we who have made it so?"

The Father looks upon them with a sweet gaze.

You will come to understand, sweet Children, that there are those forces now engaging all of Consciousness, that provide a new potential, a new opportunity.

Some will see this as very beautiful, very wondrous. Others will see it and work with it in differing ways. As you encounter these differences, know that I am with you and I am with them, and love is that which unites us. And so now you have discovered that what you felt as an absence of them is, indeed, only the absence of your love for this No-Place.

We move about from one to the other, grouping to grouping, and we strive to collect ourselves into a state of peaceful oneness. What we encounter thereafter causes us to look at one another in a manner that is new; we look at each of our brothers and sisters and we know them differently.

Then he, our brother, calls to us, "Brethren, come together. Here, I shall set this Place and we shall call it the Father's. And as it is the Father's, then, as He has said, He is here. Come, let us be one in this Place."

Instantly, we are filled with the light and peace of God, and we rejoice. No one asks. No one questions. No one seeks. For we have known now the effect of separateness, the result of not loving.

Several come together in the center of our oneness and ask gently, "Do we love our brethren in the No-Place?"

Suddenly a curious force ... a vibration ... something begins to impact our oneness. We see here and there one or more of our brethren stepping away, moving into their uniqueness, until only a small grouping in the Oneness remains.

We decide ... we *choose* to become unique again, that we may converse with those who have mysteriously moved outside of our oneness. They are gathered in a grouping, and we say unto them, "Why did you leave our oneness?"

Several respond. "Because of what was built by our brethren who brought the non-love into the center of our oneness. We do not understand and it makes us without joy."

We feel them experiencing a loss of their joy.

Instantly we surround them and embrace them, and we pour our love unto them and they accept it.

And we become one.

We move about to the vastness of Consciousness in our oneness, as though we are, each of us, being renewed ... brought back into completeness in some curious way.

Then we come to the unfolding, and here we feel the beauty and wonder of our Father dancing forth, so to say, in celebration of Consciousness ... expanding, growing, pulsing, filling us with the joy of our oneness with He.

The last vestiges of separateness fade away, and we celebrate and begin to laugh and sing our songs.

As we do, the creative colors and sounds and energies and wondrous expressions begin to mimic us and celebrate us. As we sing to them, they sing in return. We laugh and laugh, and our laughter moves in with the creation of God moving forward.

We see it, and we love its goodness ... *We love its goodness.*

A number of our brethren move back outwards in their

various journeys, singing to us as they do, and we sing unto them.

As each of our groupings move forward, we know that our joy and our laughter are bringing light to all those places that we have been to in the previous experiences, and we see how our laughter and light seem to be changing this! Even though it was in a certain manner, now it is different ... lifted up by our combined joy and song.

He, our brother, and the brethren ask us, "Let us call to the Father and have Him tell us of these, these events, these things that are occurring."

Immediately, the Father is with us.

He is nodding and smiling. Is it not beautiful, my Children? Look. You are bringing your uniqueness. And together, the beauty of your uniqueness and your joy and laughter and song ... all of these and so much more are renewing what has been for you.

He comes before the Father and asks Him, "Sweet Father, thank You for these gifts! We knew not of them before. Was it so that the appearance of that other thing caused us to discover these new gifts from You?"

The Father smiles upon him and his brethren and with a gentle humor, asks of him in return, Do you think this to be so?

Our brother looks to and fro to his dear brethren always with him, and they answer in unison, "Yes, we do, Father."

He steps back to look upon us all. Then I say unto you, my children: If you believe it to be so, it is so.

We look at each other and we begin to laugh. Our Father's words to us bring us great cheer. "Oh, Father," we ask in joyful unison, "is it so? That we can believe a thing and it *is?*"

You have seen it, have you not, sweet Children?

We look at one another and embrace each other and we laugh and answer the Father, "Indeed, so, Father."

Then know this, sweet Children: What you bring to a thing is what it becomes for you. But that thing which you bring and that which was have always been one with I. And we ... always one, together.

It is from your uniqueness, singularly and in groupings, sweet Children, that this forms, see ... forms, as you believe it to be.

We look upon one another with curiosity, "Do you say to us, Father, that this is always so?"

Always so, the Father answers.

It is your choice.

It is you who can make it so or nay.

"What if we should create a thing and find it not good, Father. What then?"

We can feel the Father touching each of us deep within in a curious way.

I have just given each of you and all your brethren another gift. It is a gift you can use to see clearly, and know that even when a thing is different, it is only that.

And you can discern it and know it, and see that it is not good or bad, but merely is. And in the essence of being, is it not so that all these things, all this be-ing, is one?

Before we can question further, the Father sayeth unto us,

Be about many joyful journeys, sweet Children. I am ever with you.

Then we perceive Him no more.

In the beginning, we begin to play and joyfully experiment and discover, and see some in our grouping begin to create things ... combinations of their uniqueness expressed in That-Which-Is, and then celebrating the beauty and uniqueness of what comes.

So, our grouping becomes one again.

We move away from these works and we move into the embrace of the All, and here we rest, contemplating, sharing, exchanging.

We call out to the Shining One and his brethren, and ask them to come and be one with us. Immediately they do so, and we tell them.

They answer gently, so beautifully, sweetly, "We know of this. The Father has given it to all of us."

"Do you do these things?" we ask.

They answer with a curious sweetness, "We do what we are, as we are, and that alone. That which is, is beautiful to us and we honor its unique beauty and celebrate that. Then we move into our uniqueness, that we each can know one another in the uniqueness of our oneness together. And we see from this the beautiful songs that come forth gently, rolling and undulating, but always in the embrace of this … the Cloak of God, as we call it."

Our brother sayeth unto the Shining One, "Do you not journey off out into the uniquenesses of creation?"

The Shining One answers with a smile, *"All of these and greater are here, dear brother. To what journey's end would we seek when the endings are here within us, and all in between?"*

Then the Shining One and those of His brethren begin to laugh.

We dance with one another, celebrating the presence of the All. We feel it. We feel it and we love it. And it cares for us and caresses us.

We say unto the Shining One, "Oh, is this not the Father, Himself?"

He answers with a quizzical smile, *"Is not all the Father?"*

We laugh and dance and celebrate all the greater. Then, we become one.

Then the Shining One and His brethren say to us, *"Would you like to share an experience with us?"*

"Of course," we answer with glee and joy.

He embraces us, with His brethren, and sayeth unto us, *"This you do not know in the knowing of yourself, but it is within you; and be at peace as I bring this knowing to your consciousness, to your awareness. All is well and at peace, and in our oneness, dear brethren, we are complete. Keep to the forefront of your consciousness this truth: We are complete."*

The rush of exhilaration as we move through the embracing All creates giggles here and there.

The Shining One smiles upon each of us and we race forward and then we begin to slow and we pause.

"We are one," He repeats. *"Say it."*

"We are one," we answer, and we laugh and our song goes forth. But curiously it stays within our *completeness*, as the Shining One has called it.

He turns us to see and He tells us, *"See in this way: that the All embraces everything. And look you, now, about."*

Suddenly, with awe and wonder and a momentary hesitation, we see that we are in the No-Place.

Several in our grouping begin to express something ... that thing again.

The Shining One speaks softly, *"Say it: We are one, we are complete."*

They do, and we are complete again, and we laugh gently.

As we look about, we see our brethren soaring about in this No-Place, busy-busy, doing this and that, seemingly to us, moving with no real joy ... something else.

He asks of the Shining One, "Do they yet do their work?"

The Shining One merely nods.

We look, and look, and see ... The Shining One has helped us to see from this completeness, and, in a time, we see its goodness: We see, these are those same brethren who are one with us, whose presence within we love and cherish. In a moment's passing we wish to rush to them.

The Shining One answers, *"We are complete. We are one. Be, unto this completeness."*

So we do.

We watch with wonder, and we move about in our completeness. We can see and feel their intentions of this work-thing. They are doing as some of us did ... They are taking their uniqueness and combining it, two portions of the elements.

We move to these and we see that there are many of them all in place, one upon the other, upon another.

Those who could not find peace and joy in being in the second element now say, "Look, you, how beautiful this is, that our brethren have created."

The Shining One turns to them with a loving smile and reaches to touch them, that they know their discovery is good.

We rejoice together in our completeness and we move. Many experiences follow ... many, many joyful discoveries, and we see that which we thought was that thing called separateness is only that which is a manner of seeing. The Shining One shows us that we can see in this way or in that way through our completeness.

And a curious thing happens ... our brethren pause in their work. There is no movement, and instantly we can hear them call out to the Father. Oh-h ... We rejoice! They are awakening from this No-Place.

The Shining One reminds us that we are complete.

In our completeness we feel the joy and warmth of the

Father's presence, and we hear Him answer their call. We marvel that the Father answers calls in this No-Place!

The Shining One reminds us that the Father answers always, wherever our experience is and whatever uniquenesses we are recognizing.

In wonder we hear them together, and we remember their sweetness. Oh-h. We look ... they are becoming one with the Father! We feel such a gladness within us, we want to leave our completeness and rush to them.

The Shining One reminds us that our completeness is good and that we are one within it, and that we are within the Father as He embraces them.

We are within the Father. We feel the Father's embrace of our brethren, and it is good. We and the Father touch each one of our brethren ... caressing them, embracing them, giving them, each, many gifts of love and joy, and His peace. And there are many, many such experiences that we share with and through the Father from within our completeness.

We marvel at this: We are within our completeness, and yet we are one with the Father! We touch them and feel the joy of knowing them in this way; and yet, here we are in the beauty and wonder of our completeness with the Shining One. We rejoice!

It comes into our knowing that this we can do: When that thing comes unto us again we can answer it and give unto that *thing* this completeness, and then the thing and we will become one with its Source. Whether within our uniqueness or without, we follow our completeness to embrace it and become one with it.

The Shining One sees us knowing this and says to us gently, *"It is the Father who has asked that I do this with you. Then, as we have done it, it is yours. This He has said unto you."*

We look at one another and begin to laugh, and we celebrate, for we know the Shining One's words are true.

Then, wonder of wonders! We hear them in their oneness, asking of the Father and we, "Help us, Father. We are seeking to create beauty in Your name. Help us to create within this Place we have made for You."

4

Completeness and Uniqueness

The wonder of our experience from our completeness brings such a joy. We see our oneness with our Father in this new way. How beautiful it is that we are complete, and in our completeness we know the Father as one.

We ask the Shining One and the brethren with Him, "How can we do this as you have done this, sweet Brother?"

"It is to be, dear friends … Be. But not to be, in the sense of a definition, but in the sense of your completeness together as one. We can do this again and again. Let us be one with our Father and our brethren."

We know this to be good. We feel as our Father feels our brethren, and we look upon them from our own uniqueness, and we see them with such a wonder and sweetness. We ponder for a moment: Here is that which we have longed for, and it has always been here.

We remember that which our Father has taught us, and we see that the *completeness*, that gift from the Shining One, gives us this wonder. We know not what it is, but we know we shall come unto oneness with it.

> *Thank you, for these works, dear Children. Indeed, you have done many good works here.*

"Oh Father, we have sought to do these works again and again, but that which we seek to express here in the nature of our love for You never forms as it is within. Show us, Father. Look within us and see this, which we hold for You. Show us the way, Father, that we might do these things."

As we watch them and feel the beauty of their intention, we are in wonder. What do they seek here? Is it not that the All embraces that which is? Yet, there is something wondrous.

> *That which is within you, sweet Children, is within I, as well. But it is you who wish it, and therefore you who have the power to doeth this thing.*

"Show us, Father. Show us the way that we can bring this from within to this Place, which we build in honor of You."

The Father looks upon them and smiles, and we feel His understanding passing all throughout us as well. We see, suddenly, the vision that they hold within, and we are in wonder of it! We know not why they wish it so, but we see that their intention is good.

Come, all of you, and be one with me. Let us look upon this, which seeks to be born from you.

The Father speaks to each of them and touches them, and they touch Him. Their oneness brings the creation from within to without. They laugh. The Father and the Children who are within this No-Place fill it with their laughter and joy.

Oh! We look upon it, for their laughter and joy is bringing forth that which is within them. Again and again we hear their laughter and feel the embrace, with them, as they embrace our Father. We begin to look here and there. For that which was within is now forming, creating, as though it was they. Yet, here they are. We are one.

Much joy and laughter transpire.

The Father speaketh His word again, and we see it gathering up all these things from within the Children of God. The wonder of it!

Here is a place, dear Children, that you can …

We struggle. We feel something different.

The Shining One reminds us that we are complete. "*We are one,*" He sayeth unto us, "*Say it. 'We are one.'*"

So we do, and the peace transforms all. Again, in the Oneness with our Father, we see this coming into being.

We hear the conclusion of our Father's loving words to them.

Here is that upon which you can create your

experiences as you hold them within. And do as we have
done, and bring them forth in the peace and joy that is
our oneness. And look you here ...

The Father points to what our brethren have called up,
and with joy we look to see the beauty!

At first we think it is the All. But no! We see radiance
here and there, and we turn to make sure our sweet
brother, the Shining One, is within our completeness. He
smiles and looks and nods to us that we shall know it is, yet,
complete.

These things, the Father sayeth unto them, *are*
of beauty and goodness. For they have been brought
from within you and we together have created it. Be
joyful and do unto these things in the goodness of our
oneness, and let us celebrate together oft here in the
beauty of that which cometh forth.

The Father embraces our brethren (and we) again.
Then He sends them forth.

Give unto this your love and your sweetness, and
remember we are ever one.

There is a rush of that thing again. Then we remember
again that our Father sayeth we need only to know it and it
becomes one with us. Together, we know the thing and
recognize that we are always one with our brethren.

We move in our completeness as we see the Father
move away.

There is, for a moment, that thing again, and we wish
for Him. Yet the Shining One touches us as the Father
does, and we know we are one.

He looks upon us with that which is unique to us.
Then, we embrace even more, and we feel our
completeness begin to move wondrously, beautifully.

We see the levels of the elements, one upon the other, beautifully structured, beautifully defined. The curiosity that we have known in the past is embraced by something we now know the Father intends for us: We *understand*.

The sweetness of the All begins to pass all throughout us and we feel the wondrous rest ... that which gives to us that which we are. We move into it and we feel the embrace of the Father all about us.

We share many experiences here, and we ask of the Shining One questions about the completeness. All the while He smiles upon us and nods.

Then our brother comes forward with his brethren. "Shining One, you have said to us that our Father has asked you to do these certain things with us. How is it that we know this not? Is there oneness with our Father that is ..."

We feel the thing stirring again, and quickly He reaches to touch that Place and give it peace.

Our brother turns to continue. "Help us to understand this. We are so grateful to You. We feel our love for You coming to the ... uttermost, to the ..."

The Shining One nods and smiles. *"You have seen it, and now you know it. And thus, your thoughts wish to speak for themselves."*

We look upon one another and we touch each other, seeking to know if one of our grouping knows this. We do not find it and so our brother asks again, "Is it in the manner that the Father has taught us? That as we believe it and as we hold that belief that it is?"

"Yes, it is the movement of our Father's gifts to fulfill the intentions of our brethren who have journeyed into that which is of wonder for they."

"We can know them. Correct?"

The Shining One nods. *"Yes. In that moment that you wish it, it is yours."*

Our brother looks this way and that with a smile and

turns back to the Shining One, "Well, then … I wish it."

The rush and movement of something within us brings us immediately to oneness.

The Shining One and His brethren embrace us and we become in that completeness again.

Immediately we know that which is the differing experiences passing by us. It is as though they move in this direction and we move in another. We find it exhilarating.

We come unto grouping after grouping of our brethren, in wondrous thoughts and experiences that they are being one with. We feel it with them and we know it, and we sense the Father with us, moving.

We turn to the Shining One, and He nods, *"Of course, it is that as we seek then He is always there. And so as we are seeking, He is with us."*

We ask the Shining One, "Can we, in our completeness, speak to the Father as we are doing these things?" We laugh together at the wonder of it all.

"Yes. Speak, then."

So we look upon one another with wonder to see if one can see the Father. We do not. We feel Him. So, we begin to laugh, and our laughter fills our completeness. We are so joyful because we are at peace in our joy, and in that moment, there is the Father … we hear His gentle laughter with us. "Oh Father, look at what our brethren are doing! Look at these experiences!"

As we continue our movement, the exhilaration grows and the Father embraces us all.

It is beautiful, He responds to us softly.

We ask the Shining One to take us to where the energies are expressing themselves.

The Father's laughter becomes very, very evident.

We ask Him, "Why does this create joy within you, Father?"

Softly, we hear Him say,

Because that which you ask about is here with you, always. It is not at the end of a past experience, nor with those of the brethren whose experiences we have just been one with.

He pauses as He watches His words become one with us.

We look from one to the other and we begin to laugh softly. For what He sayeth to us stimulates us within, and it feels good. So, we bring the laughter to the forefront to celebrate this goodness.

After some of our laughter has been complete, the Father speaks to us with such a sweet tone.

I have seen you in your completeness within the No-Place. And I have seen you bring forth love for it. Is that which was the thing that separated you now at peace?

Quickly we all answer, "Yes. It is very peaceful. We have not seen that thing for many experiences now."

The Father smiles and nods.

This is good. For you see, sweet Children, you are my Children. And that which I give to you, I give to they and all of your brethren. And as you see the others having wonderful experiences as my Word expresses itself, know that this is yours ... now ... here ... always.

We look at one another and we become one with each other, that we can know what our Father has given to us.

We gather with our brother as he asks of the Father, "Do you say to us, sweet Father, that because we believe it to be there where we first experienced it, that we also believe it is not here?"

The Father smiles and answers,
Does it not appear to be so?

We look at each other and we laugh with and at each other, for the Father's words create something unique in

63

each of us. We pause to look at each one and to touch each one and to be touched, that we are all one in the knowing of it. We turn to the Father.

He smiles ever so lovingly.

Know these things, sweet Children. Do not ask I. See for yourselves. It is there for you. If you choose it, it is yours. If you do not, it is yet always there awaiting you, seeking to bring to you the joy and wonder of my Word.

He embraces us and then He leaves in that form.

But curiously we feel Him with us.

Our brother asks the Shining One, "This is wondrous. The Father is not here, as we know Him. Yet," turning to look at all of us and we agree, and so he turns back to the Shining One, "He *is* here, isn't He?"

"Yes. He is here and always with you. But the gift that He has given to us, sweet brothers and sisters, is the gift that we might choose. He has said to us as we asked of Him that if He chooses for us then the joy is not as complete as if we choose it and know it, and come into oneness with it."

"Why, then," he asks, "did the Father come and create with our brethren in the No-Place? He did so *there*."

The Shining One smiles, speaking in a curious manner as though the Father were speaking through Him. We turn to look at one another with awe. For we cannot know for sure that it is He, the Shining One, or our Father. We are all aglow with our uniqueness as we know this thing ... We experience it.

We hear the Shining One's words and thoughts and we hear that He tells us that, *"These Children asked that the Father assist them. But they did the work together, not He alone. It was in the form of the we, the unison of God with these Children, that the work was and is done."*

Our uniqueness continues to become very brilliant, approaching the light of the Shining One but different ...

each one of us different. Oh, it is so beautiful! We cannot ask further. We must know one another.

We see now what the Father meant: that all these things are within us.

The Shining One has helped to bring them forth that we might know them. As we become one with each other, and then know the others and the others know us ... the glory of the color and the sound and the energies of the Word of God manifesting in such beauty ... we are dazzled by the presence of one another.

The awe is so magnificent that we feel something within our own being as we look upon our brethren. Then, they look upon us and we feel what they are experiencing upon us. The experience becomes unto itself, and it grows and grows, and we know that we are expanding in a way that we have not known before.

The Father looks upon us with joy and sweetness, and we know this.

We hear His words as thoughts within us.

You see? It is so.

We revel in it. The experience expands and we know it, until we reach a curious point where we feel the meaning of the completeness that the Shining One gave unto us. We feel, each of us and all of us, what the Shining One has called *completeness*. And we know that the Father is within us, not separate; and that His Word glows with the brightness and wonder of His intention for us. We see these things. Each of them and all of them seem to have beginning and ending, that we can understand them.

We hear the Father softly tell us that

This is good. Let it bring you joy and wonder, for that is my wish for you. That is my intention.

We can feel that our completeness is bringing something wondrous to us from deep within, and we knew not this place! We turn to look upon the place within us, and we see the Father!

Oh-h ... the sweetness. It *is* that it is! And we know it.

Our completeness becomes such that we and the Father are one.

With the Father, we turn to look upon those of our brothers and sisters. We see them ... all of them, everywhere. We see all the experiences, all the beauty and wonders that each are creating, and knowing.

We see the Father's Word reaching out to touch and bring something wondrous ... awareness, a sense of being to all that is. It grows.

We see it with the Father. We feel His beautiful peace. Then, we feel Him loving all of us. We feel His beautiful love for each one of our brethren.

In those sweet experiences, we, again, know each of our brethren in this way as the Father knoweth them and intends for them in their beautiful, unique wonder.

It comes to pass that we feel as though we are complete with the Father.

We feel His smile and love upon us.

We rest in His love.

Then we hear it ... so beautiful ...

But where does it come from?

We look to the Father and we see that we are separate, and yet one.

He nods to us.

Seek it out.

We know that this is who we are; this is what the Father intends.

We hear our own being calling to us.

We move unto it and we come to where we began in our completeness with the Shining One, and we celebrate with Him. We laugh and we dance as we look upon the beauty of each, as the Father seeth us.

Well, here we are with this same issue.

So much ... so many experiences become ours, and we move with ease, such ease that we have heretofore not known. We move as though we are the Father's Word. In that manner do we move.

We look upon this and that expression of His Word, and this and that creation of our brethren.

We move with the Shining One and His brethren, and we are complete with the Father.

Then, after many, many experiences, we move into the All. We become our uniqueness, and that which united us in completeness is now at rest.

The Shining One moves over, that we can see our brother and our brethren.

Our brother comes forward with his colleagues in their brilliance and light, and we admire them. He asks of the Shining One, "I see you now as I have not seen you before, sweet Brother. You are, in that way so beautiful. The presence of the Father within you brings light to you."

He turns, and we look upon each other and we see this light.

The Shining One smiles, *"You see? What you see is what you know. When you do not know yourself, then what you see reflects to you what you are."*

Our brother moves, extending himself to the Shining One, and the Shining One embraces him and they become one. We feel the love they are sharing.

Then, they call to us and we become one with them. We hold this so dear to us: It is that the Father wishes us to know each other as we know Him.

We rest in the wonder of this discovery.

The Shining One moves all about us ... touching ...

knowing us ... and allowing us to know Him.

Then, peace cometh.

We do not know how many experiences have been known during that time when we took of the peace and made it ours, but we are aware that we can know this in just an intention to do so. But we savor this time, this space, this experience. For it is creating unto itself something of magnificence that we know shall ever be ours to share.

We ask the Shining One, "May we go and share this with the others?"

We hear His laughter. *"You have already shared it with them. However, what you ask is, can you bring the knowing of it? Can you bring the knowing of it to them? It is the knowing that stirs within you."*

We look at each other in wonder, for we understand what He, our glorious Brother, means.

Then, our brother sayeth unto the Shining One with a bit of laughter and lightness, "It must be their choice to know it. It is so, correct?"

The Shining One laughs in return, *"Well done, my brother. It is so."*

He sayeth unto the Shining One on behalf of we, all of us, "You have taken something of the Father's gifts and made it your own in a manner that is so exquisitely beautiful."

The Shining One sayeth, *"It can be yours as well, if you seek it."*

He sayeth unto the Shining One, "This I know within. But I also know that it is meant for you to doeth these things. And I say to you on behalf of all of us (I speak for them as well) we ... We are ever with you."

We observe our brothers and sisters in the No-Place building upon that which they, together with the Father, have brought into being. We see them, upon the surface of the being, bringing forth that which is within them and looking upon it and choosing that it shall be or not be.

We observe them but we do not become one with them, for we feel that this is their choice. The Shining One has taught us well, these many beautiful things that the Father has given for us to come to know and to see.

So we see them together. We look in that which they call upwards and look upon the beauty of that which the Father has brought with them to shine upon them. It is as His own light, His own warmth of love that shineth upon this being. And we know its goodness.

Then, there comes upon this being the passage of the light into the embrace of something that, at first knowing, recalls to us the beauty of the All. But here and there, there are these beautiful reminders of our uniqueness upon the All, shining, glowing, each one unique and beautiful. We know, with He, that these are things that shall be, and forms of being that are growing in their wonder. We look into them and this which is the Above, and we feel the beauty and wonder as we, in our completeness, move and soar in between … looking upon them, knowing them, and laughing with them as they bring to us some good cheer here and there.

We feel the meanings that so many of these seek to give to us. They remind us of our knowings. We revel in the beauty and majesty of that which they, our Father and they, have brought into knowing. We experience it, and we know its beauty and magnificence. We give to each of these our love and we feel it reflected back to us, and we laugh and dance around each of these as we feel them respond. Beautiful.

We turn back to the Place-That-Is and we come unto it,

and we see the brethren now creating, all about, wondrous creations that, at first, we know not, for they are from deep within these of our brethren's knowing. And we are at peace with their choices and their wishes.

Then, with the Shining One before us, we move upwards through the elements and we see that others of our brethren have come to these different elements.

We look upon them and we give to them our love, and we ask them, "Are you doing a work here?"

They laugh with us. Then we know them and know their intention. They know these individual elements to be good. They have chosen to dwell in the goodness of them.

So we move to another element and find it just so.

And another.

Then we see and know that each of the elements have brought about the reflection of the elemental uniqueness unto these our brethren. It is curious to us, for the uniqueness of some of these brethren have taken on the uniqueness of that individual element in which they dwell.

We pause for a time, for our brother comes with his brethren and asks of the Shining One, "What do our brethren do here, O Shining One?"

He answers, *"Know that for yourself."*

Our brother does. Then, he turns to the Shining One again, smiling. "Will they find their way?"

The Shining One changes for a moment, then becomes as He was. *"They have not chosen. Thus, I cannot know it, lest I violate the Order of Knowing."*

Something passes through us and the Shining One feels it as well.

So we call to the Father.

The Shining One speaks, *"Father, is this as we know it?"*

The Father smiles a bit and answers with a gentle, gentle whisper of a voice,

It is.

Before the brother can ask the Father, the Shining One thanks the Father.

The Father moves back within each of us.

We pause and become one.

Then, we find the peace.

We begin to move in our completeness ... element upon element, as beautiful layers of unique color and energy and so much more. It is as though they have taken portions of the Father's Word and brought those into focus here using the beautiful colors in their individuality. Each causes a resonance within us that is, unto itself, unique.

Then, we begin to laugh and dance and celebrate as we come, finally, to our Heaven Place. We look upon one another with gladness, and we feel the love and compassion that we have embraced the No-Place with.

For many, many experiences we move about in the Heaven and see the beauty of it. We see the Father and something that He has given unto us to place here: It is His sweetness and His love. It is expressed into a new being that washes all through us and we feel the goodness of it. For a moment ... just a moment ... all of our experiences have been taken, washed from us, so to say, by this thing from the Father.

So, we laugh with our new lightness and our joy. We say to the Shining One, "Oh-h ... They shall love this Place when they come to it!"

The Shining One agrees with us.

We celebrate all the more and our experiences come back to us in our fullness. We hold the wonder of all that we know before each other, and we take of it and know it as the other knows it until we are completely one. Our laughter fills our oneness, and a delightful thing occurs ...

We begin to move.

We soar out from the Heaven Place into Consciousness.

And we can see that we are creating long, radiant spires of our laughter ... glistening, glowing, and creating a beautiful sound as we go soaring with joy and peace throughout Creation.

Then, it happens ... One of our brethren comes before us and speaks in a curious way, "You bring, here, the joy of the Father."

"Indeed," we answer. "The joy of the Father is in our completeness," and we ask of him, "What do you experience here?"

He smiles unto us, "I experience you. And I am here for you."

"What do you do?" our brother asks of him.

"I do, with you, as you do."

We look upon one another and we ask the Shining One, "Do you know this one, our brother?"

The Shining One smiles and nods. Then, the Shining One leaves our completeness and goes unto him to embrace him mightily. We hear their joy.

Wonder of wonders ... We feel the presence of the Father, growing and growing. And there He is!

He comes to embrace these two, stroking them, touching them; and they, He.

Then, they all come to us and we do the same, and we become one.

After many experiences our brother asks of the Father, "How is it, sweet Father, that we know it not in our completeness … this brother?"

The Father laughs gently.

You know him. But you know him not, because you have not called him.

"Called him?" he asked. "I do not know your intention, Father."

The Father reaches across and touches him. Suddenly, He begins to laugh and vibrate, but ever so gently. He is honoring this brother in a very special way.

We have many experiences, for the most part as we watch.

Then the Father sayeth this unto us of this, our brother:

He has chosen to be here for you in my Name. As I am within you, then he is also with you.

If there is that which you cannot meet in that which you bring forth, as you wish to build an understanding and make a way passable through it, then you can call upon this your brother and he will show you the way.

5

Lost

There come, then, many discoveries and awarenesses that we begin to share with one another, learning, as we so do, that we might grasp the consciousness of our experience in such a manner so as to reflect it to others, that they could then gift our experience with their own.

We journey, and we oft visit this Guardian, whom we love with all that we are.

We come again after many, many experiences to commune with the Shining One, and our brother asks of him, "How is it with our brethren in the No-Place?"

Many come to gather, for the bonds of oneness between us we know to be eternal and this knowing calls to each, that the sharing might be a complete one.

The Shining One sayeth unto us, *"Who will be complete with me and my colleagues?"*

We answered as one, "We shall."

In the blessing that follows we see our Father, and come unto the center of our being. We share love with one another, and He gives us His beautiful smile that we might hold this and carry it and let it be in the No-Place.

We give much attention to our completeness as we pass through the elements, exploring them, knowing them and each of us in our own uniqueness building understanding of these.

Here and there, we seek to call out to a brother. Some look upon us with a smile of warmth and love and a greeting; others look about as we pass by. But we are curious that they know us not.

We engage the No-Place in our completeness and see the goodness.

The Shining One guides us all about to feel that which is being created of the nature of the individuals' beauty. We see these things and give from our Father's smile a light of greeting and blessing.

Many who receive this look about. Some pause carefully and they close their eyes and become in oneness. But we cannot understand why we cannot be complete with them.

Our brother asks the Shining One, and we all focused our consciousness into a completeness that we all might know and understand in that same manner.

The Shining One sayeth unto us, *"They journey."*

We look to one another, that we might understand this journey of separateness. In our experience as we share this together, we had not known such.

So, the colleagues of the Shining One come and gather us up closer, that our completeness will be in harmony with these our brethren in the No-Place.

The more the Shining One explains their journeys, the more we feel it growing again, until we reach out to each other in a new way. Each of us touches the other, that the smile of the Father can be shared and renewed. The Shining One, too, pauses and gives no more, for He can see and feel that thing growing.

So we become one and call to the Father.

He answered with His sweetness,

Take my peace, my Children, and hold it before you in all things. As you come to know that which you know not, let my peace empower you, that you might transcend in the same joy as you are within, ever.

Our brother asks of the Father, and beside him the Shining One, "Is it that they wish this separateness, Father, in such a way that we must give up our love with them?"

The Father touches him so gently we can all feel it within and without, our experiences reverberating with the Color of His Word, and the sounds and beauty of Him.

Understand, my son, glancing from him to the Shining One who nods with ever so slight a smile, *that this is their pathway of choice. And as I honor their choice, you, as well, must do the same. For here, this entire Place, I have given a blessing of my Word because they have sought it. And so now I give to you, all of you, each of you, the same blessing.*

It is not a love that is lost or gone from you. It is a love that is seeking to better know itself, that in the knowing of itself and its own uniqueness, as I have gifted each of you with, the wish is within each of them that thereafter they can bring this and we all can know it as they do. But as they search, give them your love and your peace, and be joyful for them.

Some of us feel that thing as though it is rattling about like discordant color and sound.

The Father watches us with a smile and clearly understanding.

You are coming to know the structure of the No-Place, as you have called it. It is the structure of intention … the intention of all your brethren and others who know of the No-Place and who are being, even as I am speaking to you, drawn towards it. Listen. Look and see and know. Feel their intention to be a part of this.

We do feel it. We do see it like rivulets of our Father's beautiful colors, tiny rivulets, flowing. We can see them, hear them, feel them passing by.

"Are they gifting our brethren here with Your Word, Father?"

In a manner so as you understand this, yes. But even greater than this, He answers him.

And that thing continues to rattle about. Some look this way and that.

The Father smiles upon us and sayeth this,

My peace is with you, sweet Children. Look upon these things and build understanding, and know them

77

*as you would. And if you choose not, then that is my gift
to you.*

*So, as it is illuminating you within, then I am with
you to share it. And if it does not, then go in peace and
be about that which brings the joy of my Word into
being within you.*

The Father's presence begins to be covered … covered
over with this beautiful light and color! We touch this and
feel it. We love it so.

Some gather up portions and take it within their being.
And we look upon this with joy and laughter, for they create
with it, using their own experiences, in a manner of
speaking, as tools to fashion and shape the color.

The Shining One speaks very softly so as not to disturb
this. He calls to us to look out at our brethren and to feel
them, to know them.

Or brother asks, "Will we not disturb them? Will we
not do as the Father said we should not?"

The Shining One smiles with a light of understanding.
*"Remember that He said continue to give them your love and
peace, and this makes you passable to know them without any
disruption to their choice."*

As we do this we discover that much of what we see in
our grouping here in the completeness seems to be very
similar to what these our brethren are doing in the No-Place
on their journeys.

The Shining One knows, and in his knowing he calls us
to strengthen our completeness and to depart now,
straightaway.

Without a moment, we feel the effect of the elements as
we pass through them, each one glorious in their unique
expression. We see others of our brethren, very, very busy
in some of these elements. Others seem to be in a complete

state of rest. We ponder this, but we now know what the Shining One has known: that some in our grouping no longer choose this, and so we must depart and keep our completeness intact until we have made passage through the elements.

We burst unto the Heaven Place, and a thunderous expression of light and color, beautiful, dazzling. The array of combinations of sound and light, color, touch all of us so deeply that we feel certain that our Father is here feeling and experiencing this with us.

Then, the gifts of the Father manifest and we find a calm, peacefulness, a sense of very, very ... We know not what to call it. It is that which is our Father, and yet we do not see Him. We cannot touch Him, but He is here.

The Shining One gathers us together to say, *"This is our Father's eternal gift to us all, whether within the No-Place or in the greatest distant experienced. This is that with which we can ever be. And we can choose that being, just as our brethren have chosen their journeys and their busy-busy choices.*

"Come here, brethren who have felt that thing."

We watch, as a number of them step forward, and we feel that curious thing.

Our brother tells us, "Feel that which is the Father ... That which is not the Father's form, but His being, as the Shining One has told us, is ever with us," and he goes about and makes certain with each of us that we feel it and know it within, and then we know it together.

It is our Father's living light, and we love this. It brings peace. It brings a knowing that all things are aright, that all things are in the glory of our Father.

So, the Shining One is, somehow, working with our brethren who are troubled to varying degrees by the thing. We hear them communicating. *"Can you give it form, dear sister, dear brother? Can you give this thing a form?"*

They look at one another and each gives to the other

that which is their energy, their color, their sound ... their vibration of creation.

We are dazzled by the brilliance of what they share and make together, becoming one to know and express the thing. And there it is!

Many of us move back a bit, as though there is no wish that this thing moves into us, for we see the colors and hear the sound. It is a vibration that we have only subtly known ... that which we have called the thing.

The Shining One, with the thing expressed between Him and now a number of our brothers and sisters who have joined the first sister and brother, are encircling the thing.

Our brother turns to us and speaks, "Look upon this thing and let it be as it is. Let it be unto itself ... and unto itself, complete. Know your choice of it and seek that choice, ever, when you encounter this thing. For, see within it so many of the potentials, the facets of the colors, even though misshapen and dulled, are yet there. See that it could call to you. So know the truth within and hold this truth, that that of the thing cannot distort who and what you are."

The Shining One has of course, heard and known this, and we hear His consciousness speak to us, *"Hear my brother well. For this that thou knoweth is unto itself. In the order of things, as it might now be known, build understanding that this has come from the No-Place. We shall not keep it here. But know it well, for it is that which seeks to be unto itself, separate, and wishes others to join with its separateness and be that which is not. Not as an act that is,"* and he pauses in his communication, for what seems to be lots of color and sound moves by us.

Then, we hear him again, *"It is that which is, but it is not, and therefore, it is of the No-Place. It is that which can be used to create, but that creation cannot endure here any longer."*

He turns to focus upon the thing and, curiously, He begins to surround it with his brilliant light, as only the Shining One can.

We marvel at this, for it begins to move ... slowly at first, and now very swiftly, as only a line of distorted light moving back through the elements and into the No-Place. And we know it not. It *is* naught!

We look about in wonder, and the Shining One motions to us to become complete with Him and his brethren. *"Know this now, dear brothers and sisters ... that the Father's Word lives throughout all that is, and all that is not. For there is naught that is that is not of the Father. This you have known. This thing, as you have called it, is the illusion, and that illusion is within the No-Place, that those who wish to use it and create with it can do so to build the greater understanding and blessing unto themselves and others."*

Slowly at first, (and we can see he is contemplating this) our brother comes before the Shining One, and in a straight, sure communication, he sayeth ... And we cannot hear him, and so we secure our completeness and our oneness and then we hear him), "Is it not possible, sweet Brother, that these of our brethren could become complete within the illusion in the sense their belief of the illusion could make it so?"

The Shining One sayeth back, *"I think it not so; that always there is that light, see ... that which is the Father, here, in the Heaven Place, that the Father is ever, there, within them. And it is only their choice of the illusion that would make them, as you say, a part of it."*

He studies the Shining One carefully and knows his communication, and then smiles and embraces the Shining One. He gathers his brethren and we love each other completely. Then, they, together with the Shining One, move back to the Cloak of God.

Slowly, we soar off into Consciousness, the
Consciousness of our Father's Word, moving gently,
completely, undulating in a beauty and warmth that we so
love. And we move in it, giving of ourselves to it, and we
become complete with the Word of God.

We are exhilarated. We are no longer separate. The
Consciousness and uniqueness of our being has formed
into the Completion that flows into the Word of our Father,
and, though we are one, our uniqueness receives this ...
each of us, in our own manner, in our own blessing. We
come to know and understand that we can know as our
brethren have chosen, and we can journey just so in the
manner as our sweet brethren have chosen to journey. But
our love is complete, and it grows as we journey in the
living essence of our Father, which we have come to call His
life, itself. The life of God moves with us.

We have understood from the No-Place many things
that we now explore. They have created beautiful, and yet,
curious creations that have endings and beginnings. Here,
in the life of God as it flows, some of us try to do as they
have done, but here always loved and giving love. We laugh,
and we laugh, as we see the curious things that are, in
essence, born of our brethren.

Some move them about, and we move into our
uniqueness that we can explore these things. We toss them
to one another with our intention and laugh when we feel
them cascading down throughout our experiences and
knowing us as we know these creations. We are in a state of
wonder of the magnificence of our Father's Spirit ... His
life flowing and gifting us with more and more experiences,
more things to know and to become and to share.

Then, we see he who has come to be called the
Guardian, and we rush to him and give him that which we
are to give and greater. We call these experiences and offer
them to him, and he merely remains as he is. But a smile

cometh as he sayeth unto us, "That which you have done, I know. And that which you will do, I also know."

Our brother comes before the Guardian to embrace him, and so they do. And the Guardian looks upon him with a warmth, and invites him to communicate that which he knows is within him.

"How is it that I cannot bring to you, sweet Guardian, my brethren who are on manyfold journeys in the No-Place?"

The Guardian sayeth quickly back to him, "That which you say to me is naught. Why do you bring that here which is naught?"

Our brother looks about and he goes within himself to see, and he brings forth a thing and realizes that that thing is naught. And with a casual movement he casts the thing gently off into the life of our Father, and it becomes many small particles, and these become other particles, until the thing flows in the River of our Father's loving Light. His colors collect the thing and embrace each one. He turns to look back at the Guardian with a smile, and thanks him.

The Guardian only looks upon him with such a curious gaze, places a hand upon him in the expression of definition that we have come to know, and we laugh together. The Guardian tells us, "Speak these things unto your Brother within the Cloak of God. He can give you that which is the knowing of these things, if you have a wish to know them," and he laughs lightly and is gone off into the light of our Father's life, flowing through the All of Consciousness.

We marvel at this and we communicate with each other. And some in our grouping attempt to do as the Guardian has done and it makes them laugh as they seek to do this.

Then, he calls us and we become one.

In that next consciousness, we are immediately within the Cloak of God with the Shining One and His brethren.

We immediately see that many of these have changed, and several have become much brighter. Not insofar as the brilliance of the Shining One, but one who is close by the Shining One is so beautiful. As we come to know him, and we touch him and move into him and he into we, we find the joy of discovery.

Our brother comes forward with wonder, our collective wonder, and with the Shining One standing nearby, he asks of this one, "Are you as our brother, there, whom we have just been with? Are you going to become a guardian?"

We feel the joy coming from him, and from all the brethren here and the Shining One, and he affirms this.

"Will you not be with us as we move into the life of God and explore all of these wondrous things?"

Then the Shining One speaks, *"Sweet brother, he is chosen and has chosen, and thus, it is. And from this completeness of choice, he shall be the Guardian here, of what we have come to call the Cloak of God."*

We all marvel at this and we, together, question him further, "Do you not wish to come and dance in the colors and sounds of our Father's life as it flows out upon His Word? Oh, this is so wondrous!"

This one here, the new Guardian of the Cloak brightens even more and sayeth unto us, "These things I do, sweet brethren, through the knowing of it; that which you are and have done, I have done with you."

We turn to gaze at one another. We search within each other for the knowing of it.

He laughs. "See that Place?" and he comes to point to one of our sisters. "Here, know this," and he touches that which is that life of God within her.

The touch of her and He, our Father, together brings forth yet another light. And He sayeth then, "See this light?

This, I am within you," and upon saying it, that light goes back into the Father's life within her. And she begins to laugh at the experience of it.

We laugh with her and we move into oneness with her, that we might know this experience.

Many joyful experiences are shared and we come to know our brethren in the Cloak of God, in the All of God, with such completeness that we know that we are one, ever, with them.

We have come to understand that we can look upon experiences and see these as our brethren in the No-Place do: that these can be tools with which to share and build understanding, that where one has certain experiences within that the others have not in the individual sense known, then this is a reference point for us.

As we choose to know these and share our own experiences, then our consciousness grows. These things we do, and we have many such joyful times together in the experiencing of these differences, these wondrous collections of expressions of God.

Then, we come to realize and we gather together to speak of it: We wish to do this with our brethren in the No-Place. Even though we know them within, we cannot give them these gifts, for the elements seem to use that thing, that creation of separateness, the empowerment of choice that builds that thing into being.

The Shining One asks us, *Do you intend to continue to build this?*

And we realize that we are just as our brethren in the No-Place, and, as our Father has pointed out to us: giving creative life of God to the separateness that He has shown us.

Some of our grouping gather together and step forward

to say, "Is it not so, O Shining One, that we are separate?"

The clatter of energies colliding with one another all throughout our grouping requires that the Shining One do a thing and bring the Father's peace.

But there is a difference now. We all feel it. We have an understanding of something that is, perhaps, a fragment of that thing called the *illusion*, that embodies separateness to the right of choice, as our sweet Father has gifted all of us with. We can see that this discovery, this understanding, is rippling through our groupings.

Some of the groupings have moved off a bit. Some have moved completely out of the all cloak of God.

Our brother calls us, those of us that are with him, to swiftly move out to them, and he sayeth unto them, "Why do you do this thing?"

But they are so busied by experiencing the thing that at first they do not answer.

With some wonder, we look upon him as he moves directly into their grouping as an act of love.

Then, we see their grouping begin to settle and the energies seem to move to where they belong, in the order of God's life.

We move with him to embrace our brethren and we feel the effect of that thing. Some of our colors are not so vibrant. We choose, then, and become one.

We move with the life of God, hurtling ourselves, in oneness, upon the movement of God's life out into creation, and we feel the purity of His Word, the colors that flow from it soothing, nourishing, brightening. And we feel the sounds invoking energies within us. And though we so love this, we strengthen our oneness, that none in our collective groupings know anything less than the purity of the life of God, and know the vibrations of His Word resonating into and throughout our uniqueness and into the oneness of our groupings. Our completeness is such that we know not that without.

We move and flow, feeling oneness and releasing that oneness to the life of God, flowing. We become the life of God.

We move to love one another and to be loved, as our Father's love is within us. And those actions, those choices make for the greater expressions ... the far, far greater expressions than you have ever beheld before that we have within our knowing, or within our collective experiences.

It is only the voice of the Guardian that causes us to know ourselves again. It is as though the Father will call him to us, and perhaps it is so. We contemplate that the Guardian can be the Father, or the Father can be the Guardian. But there is this sweet peacefulness of being, flowing in the life of God.

A part of us wishes to answer, and so we do. We answer from the combined presence of the Father within each of us that is now freed to soar in oneness with His life.

"What do you do in the spirit of our Father?"

We hear him speak so clearly that we become startled by it and we realize that in that instant, we see each other and we laugh about this. And we come together to celebrate this knowing of our uniqueness as though it were the very first time.

And he is there, the Guardian, so brilliant, so great in his light of the Father that we rush to him ... that he (we should think) is, indeed, bedazzled by our love outpouring to him.

But nonetheless, he speaks again, "What is it that you

do? Or rather, what is it that you don't do, sweet brethren?"
He comes forward with a light so beautiful we know it is
from the life of our Father that he has taken within.

"Good brother ... We are being." (This has such a
sweetness that we have chosen it as our Father has said is
ours to do.) "Why do you ask us of this?"

The Guardian looks upon our brother with a smile that
some of us are startled, for, we think, is this not the Father's
smile? And he looks at us as we think this, and we laugh.

"If this is your choice, then so be it. Have you heard not
the calls?"

Our brother looks this way and that and pauses to be
one with the life of God flowing. And immediately we see
him start with a realization. "What is this, sweet Guardian?"

"Know it for yourself. But choose, then, upon your
knowing of it as ye would. I've come only to say unto you
that which I have said. Now it is for you to choose."

And he is gone.

We laugh about this, for when his communications are
complete, they are very complete, and we find humor in
this.

Then, we join him as we listen within the life of our
Father ... and we hear the call.

Swiftly, we become one and move towards where we
hear the call, passing through many different colors and
energies. And we realize some of these have been made into
things, and we glance at them as we move by them.
Sometimes we touch them to see their reaction, but we
keep moving until we see before us the Heaven Place.

Many of our grouping are greatly hesitant, for they
know that the Heaven Place is different. We remember our
love and that which we have placed here, and we know of
the gift of God and His life that dwells here as it does in all

of creation. But it is not we; it is that which we have given, and we love it. But the being calls to many of our grouping, and we see them and we rush to love them. But the completeness of our love cannot equal for them, some of them, the beauty and completeness of being.

As they depart back into River of God's light, we love them and we say unto them, "We shall join you again after some experiences. Be in our love until that time, sweet brethren."

We decide to become complete, and in our completeness we move into the Heaven Place and we see some of the beautiful brethren who are in the Cloak of God with the Shining One.

"Why do you dwell here?" our brother asks them.

"We have chosen it," they answer. "Have you heard not the calls?"

And we turn to hear, and we hear the calls!

"What is this?" our brother asks of the brethren.

One of the brethren moves gently and sweetly up to him and touches him in the foreknowledge of the impact of his communication. "They have lost their way."

The intensity of the energy of this communication is such that we cannot immediately balance with it.

We come together in a degree of completeness that is the very best we know to do. And we bring the life of our Father from within each of us and place it to the forefront of our being, each of us.

Then cometh the Father's peace.

Then, we ask, "Father, how can this be?"

6

A Caller Stirs

The impact of the discovery that such an event could be brings the consciousness of all us into a state of, at first, disarray ... with the movement of something that has not been seen nor known.

The calling forth unto oneness brings the familiar unanimity, and the sense of peace and joy that comes with oneness brings all things into order and joy.

Then, he, our brother, Yo-El, speaks on behalf of all. "Father, we are knowing this thing that is, as you have called it in past, a *separateness*. But here, Father, we call upon thee."

The Father answers,

I am with you, as always. What do you question? What is it that you seek? For within is that which is unto every need, complete. It is I within you. And this you know.

"Teach me Father that I might better know this ... I and my brethren, as we are now one. We have heard this call and we have come here, to the Heaven Place, and the brethren of the Shining One have conveyed to us that some in the No-Place call out. Do they not know, Father, to call out to Thee?"

Many things have changed in the progression of their choices, dear brother and sister mine. And this I say to you in the form of He who is the Shining One, (who shall join you very soon) that you might know that I and He and my spirit are all throughout.

It is the knowing of this and the choosing of it that is all that is needed. Therefore, what you ask of me, sweet son, is the same as you would ask of the Shining One and of my Spirit.

Know this to be a truth, for much lies ahead wherein if you can make this known unto yourself, ever shall it be present for you, no matter what is the experience encountered. No matter what gift you seek to give, know this and you shall ever be free in the knowledge of it.

In our oneness we contemplate that we see the Father, and we know the Shining One speaks! And we know this, the eternal ... the *Eternal!* We pause to contemplate this!

And the Father answers us,

It is my living Word that you seek to find definition for. It is ever with you. It is that that gives life and yet it allows you to be free, and from that, to choose.

Some will say to you this or that, but ever know this in your completeness: I am ever with you.

"Why has the Father left us?" one asks our brother.

Yo-El answers, "Did you not hear? He just sayeth unto us that He is ever with us. I know that as I asked of Him, this He gave. Therefore, it is a truth to be lived. Look within, sweet brother, and see for yourself."

Yo-El realizes that something, yet again different, is occurring ... that the one who has asked of him cannot find it within his being. Yo-El moves to him and touches him and gains his acknowledgment, that he can embrace him, and Yo-El feels the reaction, as the one who is seeking tries to know *What is it? Where is the Father within me?*

Yo-El touches him, and that one feels with his consciousness where he has been touched. "I do not ... I do not know Him there within me."

Yo-El touches him again, but this time he has called his brethren to surround them in a oneness, he and this one who seeks in the center. And Yo-El calls out.

Then cometh the Guardian, Michael. "What seek you, brother?"

"Help me, dear one. Help me to help this, my brother, who cannot find the Father within."

Michael comes behind and reaches around to embrace them both. "Give him thy truth again," sayeth Michael.

Yo-El does so … gives him his truth, just as the Father has given it to them. And he feels the one seeking quiver.

Then there is peacefulness.

All can feel it. All know it.

Michael turns to look at us all, still embracing us. "Know this and hold it within you, and it will serve you well in those times which lie ahead. For I see you and I see that which stirs within you … we all know the calls. Be of consciousness that this is thy gift, given to thee by the Father."

Slowly, Michael releases them and rises up to be gone.

Yo-El looks at the one who was questioning, and he sees that one's light. He looks to the left and right and up and down, unto the forefront and behind … All places looks he to see, and then he knows that it is a good work … that that thing which has a different shining is not present.

All of us who had encircled them, rush to embrace them, and then they move just a bit, that we might dance the dance of oneness and love. We swirl about, touching one another, knowing one another, and becoming one, bringing forth the colors of the Father's creation and calling it to be one with us. And so it does. And the beauty and wonder of the light and color and sound fills the area in which we have chosen to dance.

Some of those of the brethren of the Shining One leave the Heaven Place to come and be with us in this dance.

Then, Yo-El calls us, "Let us turn to find more of this strangeness … this call."

So we move back into the Heaven Place and feel the glory of the love and compassion that fills the Heaven Place. It bathes us, and we give unto it that which we have to give of our uniqueness.

The brethren of the Shining One gather around.

Yo-El speaks to them, "Of what nature is this call? How can they can be *lost*? They are in the No-Place, are they not?"

The brethren of the Shining One speak softly, "They are."

"Why do they not simply leave?"

"They have built that which is of their choice, and they have built a belief in it of such power that they have chosen to dwell within the power of their own choice and belief. And they have made it into what could be called (by the measure they use) near perfection."

"What is this thing they call *perfection*?" he asks.

A brother of the Shining One smiles broadly, "You shall have to see for yourself. We have no way to tell you other than to say it is not in the No-Place. It is a no-thing. It is that they have built," and he turns to the other Shining brethren, and they help him. And he turns to continue on, "They have built places, places within the No-Place. Each has unique qualities, and each has unique essences, and on, and on,"

One of those with Yo-El comes forward and sayeth, "Is it like the elements?"

He answers, "Yes, very much so, but in a way that is in a *place*.

"A place? What is a place?"

"It is a confinement of one's wish, one's thought, one's love."

Then we remember our works with taking the colors and those whom we had seen in consciousness building the beautiful shapes and forms of the colors of the Father's Word. "Then, why do they call us?"

The brother who speaks to us shrugs, "They call us because they cannot find their way out. They are lost."

We begin to move this way and that, and some begin to send off little rivulets of different colored lights. So Yo-El calls us into oneness, and peace begins to transform us into ease. We all share the consciousness together and turn to question further. "Then the call is to the Father?"

"No," the brother shakes his head to and fro in a manner that is of the nature of their forms in the Earth.

"What is this that you do?"

"It is that which they do. They have chosen it as an expression."

Looking up and down the brother of the Shining One, Yo-El smiles, for he sees the nature of this to be of beauty.

And then, the brother is the light of his uniqueness again.

"Show me again, please."

So, the brother does.

We all look with wonder.

"And this they have created as well?" asks Yo-El

"It is so, and so much more."

"How have they done this? We were just with them."

"No," the brother answers. "No. You do not understand, and I cannot give it to you. You need to *know* it. Do you wish to become complete?"

"Indeed," Yo-El responds.

So all of the brethren of the Shining One gather together, and they become complete.

The brother leads us past an element, and another, and another.

"Many such now exist," Yo-El comments to the brother.

"Indeed."

Finally, we are within the No-Place. We marvel at the beauty of the forms and expressions that have been utilized here.

"They have done some very beautiful forms, some very beautiful things."

The brother only acknowledges Yo-El, and we continue to move. We move through the colors and forms and we pause here and there to know the various expressions and aspects, and the choices and the compounding of choices ... most unlike anything that has been known by us, and we move further and further into the breadth and depth of the No-Place.

We look, to see some of our brethren whom we know from beyond the No-Place!

Some in our grouping wish to go to them, but they are told to remain in the Completeness.

"Here is one," the brother shows us.

"What is he doing?" Yo-El asks of the brother.

"He is being lost."

This creates such a rush of awareness within our grouping that we all struggle to sustain our completeness, and it is visible to us in our consciousness that this disruption in our completeness causes an immediate reaction, outwardly, in the No-Place! We feel a strangeness, as though something is pushing on us, all about us.

The brother of the Shining One calls out, "Speak your completeness ... *now!*"

And we all speak our completeness, and the sweet calm and tranquility of the love of God fills us.

Yo-El moves to the center. He reaches within, and he brings forth that of the Father's promise and holds it forth.

We all feel it. We all know it to be the Father's Word, and we are in-filled to our completeness. We look about with our consciousness and all in the No-Place has returned to its normalcy, as it was.

The brother of the Shining One sayeth to us, "We leave now. Move with me."

We feel the changes. We know the structure that has been created, and the memory of the forms and shapes and so much more is held within our being.

Some of the elements seem to resist us, and the brother of the Shining One moves about swiftly, touching us all, and we all feel the blessing of the Shining One, and we move again with ease, until we have reached the Heaven Place and we become unique.

As soon as we do, some who had for so long been journeying with Yo-El say to him, "Our love is forever with you. This you know. But we choose not to be there, and so we now depart."

Immediately they are gone!

All of the remainder become jostled by the change in energy of their oneness.

Yo-El calls to us and sayeth unto the brother of the Shining One, "We shall return briefly."

And he acknowledges, for he knows.

Yo-El calls us into oneness and off we soar, turning this way and that, knowing one another, feeling the wonderful and enduring essence of the Spirit of God within us as the Father has given it ... His Word within as a living thing, a spirit. We know this Spirit and we embrace it, and we become one with it.

The Father speaks to us in our oneness,
You have learned a great deal.

One steps forward to the Father and sayeth, "Father, if they call, do they call to You or us? Why did You not just speak to them?"

There is a pause that is curious to all here.

The Father speaks in a loving whisper,
They have chosen it. And it is ever their right to choose and know this thing that one of you has created, called separateness.

That one begins to flourish with color and sound.

The Father touches him and whispers with

lightness of being and word,
> *Be light within. Hold my truth within you. For this is only a thing. It is only that which is used to define. Is it not?*

The brother, feeling the love of the Father's touch upon him, realizes this and gives thanks to the Father.
> *When I say to you, you have created it, it is in the discovery of a thing that it comes into being. Is it not, sweet son?*

Very quickly we all realize what the Father sayeth ... that if we know it, then we can speak it, and in the speaking, it is just as He: It is created.

We become so filled with rejoicing at the knowing of this that we embrace the Father, and we give Him our completeness.

He embraces us with His completeness and we become one with the Father ... and we are one with the Father!

We pass through many things, seeing them as the Father sees them, knowing them as the Father knows them. It fills us with the goodness of our Father to know these things.

When we realize that, here with us is the Shining One and the Father, and the Father's Word and light, which we know to be His living Word, His Spirit. And we surround these with our love and our completeness. And we *know* them.

We feel the oneness and the peace and completeness of being, and we see all else to be as it was ... but not ours, merely those things. We know them because we have known them in the personal and we have known them as a group. Now, we know them with the Father and the One of light, and the Word of God eternal ... the living Light of

Him. In our oneness with the Father, we look out into the All, and we feel the warmth of its embrace as the expression of our Father. And we look beyond, into the Consciousness and we see the dazzling glory, the wonder, the majesty, and the unfolding jubilation of expression ... so awesome!

We are in-filled with joy to behold the Word of God, our Father, going forth, touching all, giving life.

We turn to embrace our Father and we awaken our oneness, and we feel something wonderful ... We feel the undulation of Consciousness, the vibration of the expression of our Father's Word moving, rising and falling, soaring and rising and gliding into the All, touching it and moving, great, soaring, wondrous bands of the Father's Word expressed in light.

We move out upon it. We cannot resist the pull of this, and we are all together and we laugh and we dance upon the undulations. The vibrations are so beautiful! We feel them. We take them into our being. We share them with one another from ourselves and from without.

Then, we see ... The Shining One moves off a bit and shows us another such wondrous undulation, and then another.

Then cometh Michael to show us others.

We see how they move and how they intertwine with one another, and where they do, glorious bursts of light, expressions of the Father's Word, take form and bless everything with His sweetness.

We rush into these to feel them. It is as we have felt our Father, but in a different way. Something that is expressed from Him and yet it is He.

So many experiences follow and here we are in the completeness of our Father and His shining spirit, and our beautiful Shining Brother. We are complete.

Then it comes to pass that we look to see the Shining One has moved off into the All. He has left his trusted Guardian, indeed one anointed by the Father (and his own choice) where he serves to preserve the beauty and to give to those who seek it, and to keep it in its pure form.

Yet, we remain within the Father.

It comes to pass that Yo-El moves out and begins to move further towards the No-Place.

We say to ourselves within the Father, "He must be seeking to answer the call." And we say to the Father, "Are we ever one with You?" We know His answer, and we strive to make this a part of our being. We give our love to our Father and tell Him that we shall leave a trail of light between Him and we, and we move out immediately to be with Yo-El again.

We are here, in the Heaven Place, and now it is different. We feel the beauty. We feel the sweetness of the love and compassion as we have placed it here, we and our brethren. We pause to remember them and we feel them acknowledge our remembering, and we know that they are upon their choices. But their love is with us.

We move very swiftly to know the Heaven Place completely, and we know that it is a promise of sorts … something that remains here eternally: that no element can deny those who seek it; no choice can impart a limitation to it; and those who choose to be here are free. And we contribute to the power of our original love and compassion.

Yo-El tells us, "Give to it the freedom of God."

So we do.

We send forth our knowing of those who call unto us.

And we feel that some are stirred by it!

So, Yo-El calls us to come into a completeness.

We do, and we begin to journey as we have been shown in past. We pass through the elements, and another, and another and soon we are within the No-Place.

We see it as we have seen it with the Father, and we honor it, as does the Father. We see the structure of it and we reach out to know it, but we do it from our completeness, not from our individuality. For, were we to do so, we would leave the completeness and we do not know what would occur thereafter. We presume we would simply seek to become one and then seek for completeness. But we do not know this.

Yo-El leads us up to the immediacy of one who is calling.

We look upon this Caller, and we say to him from our completeness, "Knowest thou not we are here?"

We see the Caller stir, stir in the No-Place consciousness that they have created.

But the Caller does not answer.

We call again, "Know us. We answer your call with the love of the Father."

This time this Caller stirs and we see tiny flashes of light. And we say to each other, "Look! He stirs."

Yo-El calls us to our completeness, that we attend to this. We do, but we are renewed in our joy. So we call to him again, "Our love is here for you. Know us."

And the Caller stirs!

This time great bursts of light go this way or that and one of them strikes the periphery of our completeness.

Yo-El connects with it, and instantly the Caller is within our completeness! We nearly come unto that uniqueness of our individuality, and we all work with each other to re-energize, renew, our completeness, and we begin to move.

Yo-El guides us through the elements and we feel jostled, buffeted. He moves to the center and brings forth that truth, and we become strong in our completeness, and we rise up into the Heaven Place.

Yo-El sayeth to us, "No. Go beyond."

So we burst forth into Consciousness and we feel the flow of energy, of light, of sound, of color, of creation, coming to us in the Word God.

We all want to rush to the Caller.

But Yo-El sayeth unto us, "Be at peace. Look upon him. He is not yet of his own being."

So we give to him our peace and our love. Oh-h ... We ache to be one with him. Suddenly, we realize that we taste something, and we know that it comes from the Caller.

Yo-El sayeth to us, "Retain our completeness whilst I journey to him. In our oneness, I shall do what I can. Are you with me?"

We tell him we are complete with him.

At first, the Caller is difficult to distinguish, in terms of who he is.

So, Yo-El reaches within himself to know the Caller as the Father knoweth him. Yo-El brings this knowing and he holds it forth. As the shining of that truth of the Caller's uniqueness begins to touch him, he becomes more and more complete, and the energies begin to move in greater and greater harmony within and about his being. The colors begin to become strong and vibrant. They take on the hues of the Father's Word, and the sounds are now present to behold, and they do not cause one to wish one to go elsewhere.

A small communication can be heard. "Is it you, my

brother?"

Yo-El responds with joy, "It is not only I, but all of your brethren. Look you!"

We can feel his joy pulsing off of us. Each one of us feels it as though he has touched us, and we feel another thing. So it goes for quite a time, and many things are given to us by the Caller.

We move off into Consciousness.

But Yo-El leaves us, telling us to go to where the Guardian is and that he will join us.

So we do.

He moves back to the Heaven Place and comes to be with those who are the brethren of the Shining One. He gives to them that which we know and that which has been given to us by the Caller.

They come together and call out, and the Shining One comes and they become one. The rush of beauty, life, and sweetness pass through all.

Then we become our uniqueness that we can, in this Place, speak to the Guardian and tell him of these things, and we come to know that he has known them.

He sayeth, "Do you not remember?" He smiles brightly.

We laugh at this because it is something that they do in the No-Place: They choose to remember ... or not! So we laugh with him.

So it goes.

When Yo-El returns to us, he tells us that we can know

that the Shining One has sent His love and blessings, and so he touches himself and opens this, that we can be there with him, where he was. We move into those colors of the Word of God that bring peace and renew, and we let this bring our completeness back to its original form, for we have come to realize that our experiences in the No-Place gave unto us many gifts, but now that we know them, we choose them not. These colors of the Word of God bring to us our renewal, and we are joyful

The Caller now is complete, as well, and he shares with us many things and we come to understand so much that has been created in the No-Place: Others have taken those creations and altered them, and they have come into the state of completeness with their creation so that others cannot know what they have created. We realize that the elements are, indeed, something of this nature, though we know not yet how that is.

So now we have the knowledge of the No-Place and of those things which they have manifested, and that which can bring about a limitation such that they know not their own nature and that they come unto that Place from whence they call ... that Place wherein they are lost.

We learn from him that they, at first, intended to remember the Father and celebrate each new creation, each new manifestation and discovery. But that curious things happened ... that, as the influences of other discoveries had affect upon theirs, they created reactions and such to preserve themselves, and those impacted others who responded in much the same way. And we find that they created something that came to be called *competitiveness* ... that one would seek to make a creation or express a thought-form, an intent, and make it (by their definition) greater than the others ... and from this, energies, convolutions of the colors of creation believed by them to be beautiful for they saw themselves as the creators of it.

But here, in the pure colors of God, we know these to be expressions of ... expressions of being separate from God! The realization of this is stunning to us, and we swiftly gather the colors of the Father's Word, and have these pass all throughout us.

Yo-El calls us together, and he reaches within to bring that gift of the Father. And as he does, we all remember it and bring it forth.

The Father sayeth unto us in profound sweetness and love,

Blessings, my Children.

The Caller is jubilant and rushes to be one with the Father again.

We hear and feel him doing one of those things from the No-Place ... It is called weeping, and we hold onto one another tightly, that we can honor them, and we hear their communication.

The Father sayeth to him,

I know these things, sweet son. I have always been with you. It was only the choices, not I, that made the distance seem to be so.

But look, you are here. You remembered and you called out. And these, your sweet brethren, came to you. And now we are one again.

We burst forth in joy and oneness, and the Father with us, and we soar off here and there to the All and bask in the beauty of it, and back into Consciousness, and race out to dance upon the expression of our Father's Word as it unfolds before us in the joy and wonder of His beautiful creation.

Many experiences pass.

And then, in the peace and tranquility in the midst of Consciousness, the Father sayeth,
Be about those things that are joyful to you. And, as you choose, it is your right; as you believe, you create. Remember this.
But remember always that I am with you.

There is a curious feeling of longing, one of those things from the Earth-planes, the No-Place consciousness, and within it, that sphere that they call home. We ponder for a moment, *How can they believe this?* And yet, we see the beauty of their intent and we honor it.

We look at the many memories that the Caller has given us and we study these carefully, and the wonder of how our brethren made manifest something from nothing and made it live, gave it life! How, in the making of these things, and the breathing of life into them, they did not share the goodness, the beauty and the uniqueness, with each other, but sought to place these in small places where they could be preserved, where the intent was that this would be forgotten.

"No," the Caller tells us, "it is not that way. They simply wish to believe themselves to be that which there is, and their creations to be of greatness."

We seek this out among the many things He has given us, and we see that they have belief that some are actually better than others! And we marvel at this, and we look at each other and we laugh for a great time of laughter, and we realize that they believe these things!

The Caller tells us, "Oh, it is believed to near completeness. I tell you, all of my being had to summon forth the memory and to reach out in a call in the hope that the Father would remember me."

"You remembered the Father?" Yo-El asks him.

"I remembered something ... and we gave it a name, those of us who believed this. But we had to use care, for those who did not wish us to believe that which was beyond creation would gather up together upon us, and we could not muster sufficient to resist, and, thus, we would become theirs."

Jolts and rivulets and pops and all sorts of curious happenings of the energies of our uniqueness ... each one cascades off in this distance and that and bumps into each other and creates sounds and colors.

Yo-El calls to us to become one. He calls forth the peace of God and we all reach within to bring it forth and we are at peace. He turns to us and reminds us that the Caller is merely sharing, that we have the choice to share at depth (in other words, to live it) or to share to the extent of knowing it. He asks of us, "Do only this, brethren ... Merely know this. See it, look upon it and know it. But do not live it, do not be it. Lest we create another No-Place here."

We all laugh mightily, and we embrace each other and spin about in a glorious dance of love and hopefulness.

The experiences conclude, and Yo-El asks of the Caller, "Does this occur?"

The Caller does that thing they call sadness. We feel it, but we choose not to be it. And he responds, "A little. It is starting, I fear. Did you not hear other calls?"

We did. We tell him that we did, and he tells us more and more.

Some in our grouping take on a certain color and energy of their own. They move off to the side and they state to us, "They cannot do this to our brethren. It is not in the Righteousness of God!" They begin to become one in such a manner that they are one with their own belief and choice.

Yo-El calls us into oneness and we swiftly move after them, but they are moving in their own choice.

The Caller, in our midst now, states, "They are answering. They are being pulled into that which is the creation."

Yo-El calls out strongly, "Father, help us to help our brethren."

We hear Him gently say,
They are not in need. They are merely choosing.

Yo-El softly answers, "Thank You, Father. They are going to be in the No-Place, aren't they?"

The Father answers not, but we can feel it.

Then, to our joy and surprise, in the midst of our being, is the Shining One! He sayeth unto us, *"It is their right to choose."*

Yo-El is touching the Shining One, and they share their love. Then he moves off a bit and states, "Why? Why is it their choice to become as the others?"

"No, it is not that. They wish to, you call it ..." turning to the Caller who is in awe of the Shining One, *"you call it, being saved. They are going to save the remainder of the Callers."*

Many experiences pass. The Shining One has returned to be in the All. And we hear our moving. We are seeking to find that Place of gladness and joy, and we come to embrace Yo-El. And we all feel it.

The Caller, who is greatly loved now, sayeth unto us, "Do not give it life. If you give it life, if you give it your thought, it will be within you. I tell you that it grows with a curious nature! It seems to be of itself, unique, and yet you come to know it is within you, not without, and the more you seek to bring it separately, you realize that it is something you have allowed to be within you."

Yo-El seems to brighten a bit, shrugging off that thing, as the Caller has said it.

We all are more joyful in the Father's light as we realize that we might have created another No-Place. With this, we laugh mightily and we call to oneness and we spiral off into the glory and wonder of the colors of our Father's Word.

We pass by the Guardian, and he gives us love, and off we soar. We rest in the peace of God and the glory of His Word unfolding. But all of us have a knowing within ... that a great part of our joy, our love and our beauty, is now in the No-Place.

7

Lines-of-Light

It is, indeed, a momentous time for us, as the Caller brings to us the fuller understanding. As we become one with him, we can know his experiences to such depth that many of us need to pull back because the being in it is against our true joy and, thus, we choose it not in its completeness.

The Caller comes, again, to each of those and sayeth unto them, "Look you, then, and know it. You needn't be one with it to know it."

So they do, and now we are whole, knowing that Place and all the structures that are a part of it, at least that is our cognition of it ... our, as he has called it, *thinking* of it (which we find a delightful humor).

We never tire of exploring and being one with our Father's Word as it goes forth, and we can feel the essence of His profound love and the manyfold gifts as we soar along, carried by the wonderful rush of His love in the form of His Word.

The many, many experiences pass us by and we come to that place wherein Yo-El states to us, "Let us move to the Guardian. I wish to be one with Him for a time."

There is that which continually calls to us, though in a loving way, that some truly find it difficult to leave God's Word moving forth.

So Yo-El goes to them and they become one, and he gives to them of his true love and all that he is.

So they remain and we move to the Guardian.

He gives us great love and peace as we come into his being. There is a time wherein we share and he tells us of many things.

Yo-El comes forward and sayeth unto him, "Michael, my brother, I wish to know more things."

Michael smiles his love upon Yo-El and laughs softly.

"What things do you wish to know? Do you feel that you are absent of some of the *things*, as you call them?"

"No, no," Yo-El responds, smiling with his beautiful light. "No, I do not wish to know of the things. I wish to know more as God's Child."

"Then why do you not seek your Brother?"

Yo-El studies him for a moment and looks about, and realizes then that he speaks of the Shining One. "Can I not call Him?"

"You can," Michael responds. "Indeed, He knoweth of this conversation, yet can you not realize a truth?"

"And that is what?" questions Yo-El, smiling, knowing that this is just what he has asked for.

"Go to Him and ask Him to share that with you and so much more. I leave you now," and he is gone back to his position in the beauty and wonder of consciousness, and the raiment of its expression moving about and touching all that is.

Yo-El is smiling very broadly and calls to us, "Let us be in oneness."

So we become one.

The Caller moves to be immediately beside Yo-El and Yo-El looks upon him with a gladness within, for this is that brother who was, as they call it, lost and is now present with us in his fullness.

We pause a moment to look upon the Caller and love him. His beauty is so exquisite.

He knoweth this and responds, "As are each of your uniqueness, equally so, beautiful."

Yo-El then calls us to become complete, and we move with joyful ease and exuberance and exhilaration passing through us as we move past the presence of other brethren, who call out to us with joy and who show us the beautiful collages of color that they have taken from the Word of God and then they dissipate them, that they can be free.

So it goes, and we come to the All.

We pause to honor it for a time, for as we stand here where the Consciousness and the All embrace one another there is such a beautiful sense of balance and completeness, harmony and symphonic joy of color and light and sound and vibrations that seem to be joyful to be with one another.

Oh, we love this! And it, in turn, loves us back.

Then the Shining One is in our midst with joy for us all!

Yo-El goes to Him to embrace Him on behalf of all of us, and the Caller goes with him to do the same. And He gathers us all into oneness that we might all embrace each other and be one.

Oh, it is so wonderful.

Some experiences are had by us and then we move into the All and are greeted with great exhilaration and joy by all who accompany the Shining One. As they gather around us we celebrate that their number has grown mightily.

Then we come to that place that the Shining One has called for us to gather about. *"What seek you, my brother?"* smiling, for all know that He indeed knows just what Yo-El seeks.

Yet we also know now, as the Father has shown us, that when we know a thing, the speaking of it begins its birthing.

So, Yo-El smiles and laughs. "I wish to know and understand. I cannot say to You, sweet Brother, what that is. Yet, we have all shared this, and I speak on behalf of all my brethren gathered here. Teach us, sweet Brother. Teach us."

The Shining One comes to the center of our grouping and touches the Caller and Yo-El, and they reciprocate and make a little symbol, a little form. And where each of them are, are three points.

Then, without comment, three of the Shining One's brethren come forth and make another triangle that becomes one with the first.

He sayeth unto Yo-El, *"See this? That which our light and our being manifest?"*

Yo-El looketh upon this and answers, "I see it, but I do not comprehend Your meaning."

"This is the teaching," the Shining One sayeth to him, and He steps forward.

To our delight, we see His light remains in that place!

He extends Himself to our brother, Yo-El, who moves immediately to be one with the Shining One. Again, in his place, remains the brilliance of his light, as though he were yet there! This brings us all great wonder and joy.

Then, the Shining One makes Himself and Yo-El one and they begin to move, and from our place they move up from us.

He sayeth to Yo-El, again, *"Do you see this?"*

Yo-El looks upon it from apart from where he was and he is enamored with this. "What is that where I was?"

"And that is you," responds the Shining One without a moment's pause, as though to continue His own statement.

They look, and the Shining One moves him back to the center of the grouping that he can look about.

Yo-El moves about to where he had been originally and he feels himself. He turns, again, to walk back to the Shining One in the center, and this time it is he who becomes one with the Shining One, and he intends to move upwards, and so he does.

We all begin to celebrate this with great laughter and joy, and they return to our grouping.

Yo-El continues, "Is this that which stirs within me?"

"*It is a part,*" responds the Shining One.

"Show me, Brother. I seek it. It is that as the Father has taught that, if I place it before myself as that which I intend and then I," turning to the Caller, he smiles, and then turns back, "*choose* it, then it begins the process of coming to be born into our consciousness, our oneness, with You, here, in the All."

Now the Shining One sayeth no more but comes and calls Yo-El to the center, and they become one.

They move and they move, and soon we see them not! We cannot perceive them! We can feel their spirits, for we know we are one with them. We look to the right and left and we see their light remains. How beautiful! And these forms begin to glow and pulse. It is magnificent.

"Where are we?" Yo-El asks of the Shining One.

"*We are in the No-Place.*"

At first Yo-El begins to exhibit some responses to the knowledge, the consciousness, the words, *No-Place*.

The Shining One smiles at him, "*You have learned something from the Caller, and when you are complete with remembering it, then we shall continue.*

Yo-El smiles, but does not laugh, for he respects the Father's Word, that they should do naught in the No-Place to disrupt anyone or anything.

The Shining One knoweth this and He sayeth to Yo-El, "*This is not the same, my brother.*"

"In what way?"

"*It is that you are not in that same expression, but you are in that which is the Word of God within you.*"

Yo-El becomes calm and quiet as he allows this thought-form, this expression, here in the midst of the No-Place, this beautiful truth given to him by his brother.

"Is this the same, sweet Brother, as when the Father sayeth *'I am always with you'*? Is it that Force?"

"It is of the Father and, therefore, it is that same Force, my brother.

"Are we as we are in this Force ... Are we in this Force with God?"

"Ever," He sayeth in a whisper of love.

Yo-El looks about and he cannot perceive the Father.

The Shining One smiles on him and tells him to think of the Father and naught else, which he does, and in a moment the Father is there with them and they are all together, one touching the other and each one touching.

The Father sayeth unto Yo-El,
My Spirit has stirred within you, sweet son.

"Oh Father, this is so beautiful and yet we are here, in the No-Place. And they know us not?"

No, they would only know you were they to be in their spirit.
But ... You see?

We look about and they are very busy, some creating different things which Yo-El does not recognize.

He asks the Father, "Do they continue to do these things here?"

The Shining One answers for the Father, *"Ah, yes. They continue, and much more will come."*

"Can I know where my brethren are who have come to this place? Are they ..." and he casts his consciousness all about. "Are they here?"

The Father intercedes and sayeth,
You and your brother continue this journey of joyful discovery. I am ever with you.

The Shining One begins to move slowly across the

117

expression of the No-Place.

Yo-El looks upon it with wonder. "What are these things that they have created?"

"*Ah! There are many, and soon enough I believe you will know them.*"

Yo-El ponders this but he questions not, and there, just a distance away, he immediately recognizes those of his grouping who had come to this No-Place to answer the calls.

The Shining One studies him carefully. "*You are doing very well, my brother, for I tell you, were you to seek now to do a thing (as they call it) we would be back in that form from whence we have come.*"

"What is the difference?" Yo-El asks.

"*It is that this is that expression of the Father and, therefore, this expression is the Father in our uniqueness. As you look about and see, you will recognize the energies, the expressions of the Father's Word that have been called together here by those who began the No-Place, and others who have come to it since. And I will show you something very beautiful ...*"

He becomes very, very complete with Yo-El in a manner that is so incredibly freeing that Yo-El feels as though he is naught. Then, he feels the Shining One in the presence of the No-Place, moving all throughout it. In every thing and in every place he feels, as he passes through it with the Shining One, that he *is* that thing, he *is* that place.

They have many experiences. Then the Shining One takes him back to be just above the more dense energies or vibrations in the No-Place, up above these in the place where some aspect, some energies of the Spirit of God are present but are only with boundaries that are of the outer No-Place, itself. He and He and Yo-El soar through this and they see it to be beautiful.

"This feels to be something different than the other energies."

The Shining One sayeth to him, *"You will come to know this. This is that which helps them to be in their form, that helps them to be one with their spirit. Come, and know this next ..."*

They come to a beautiful, wide expanse and they look upon it and see it to be beautiful.

The Shining One gently soars downward, into it.

As they engage it, Yo-El expresses a comment of delight, "This is like the Father's smile. This is like His joy."

"Indeed."

As they move through the great sea, they discover many things. They see some very pleasant light just ahead and the Shining One calls him to pause. As they observe this they can see the light from the Father's Word that has been given form and definition. The light is moving and undulating in such a curious way.

Yo-El asks, "What is this?"

The Shining One sayeth to him sweetly, *"This expression of the Word of God is creating itself again."*

Yo-El studies very carefully and after a bit he is in wonder as he looks to see several smaller lights seem to have broken free from the larger light.

The Shining One sayeth to him, *"This is a part of their works that they have engaged in. Some have loved their creations so very much that they did not wish them to not-be, were they not giving them their spirit, their light. So they called upon the Forces of the Word of God to form in a way that these could know themselves to be that form, and to repeat itself. It is beautiful, just beautiful."*

They move with a swift gentleness to view more such lights in different places as the brethren of the No-Place have created it.

Then, they move back. *"Here are your brethren from your grouping."*

Yo-El looks upon them and knows them, but they look and feel different. "They do not know I am here?"

"*No, they do not,*" responds the Shining One.

"Do they not know this form?"

"*Not yet,*" responds the Shining One, "*until a teacher comes to them.*"

"What is this thing you call, a *teacher?*"

"*It is one who will come to them and move to be with them and show them, as I have shown you, and the Father has shown me and my brethren.*"

"Are your brethren coming here?"

The Shining One nods an affirmation. "*In a time, yes, to be here.*"

"May I move close to them?"

So they do.

Something within Yo-El changes. It moves in a curious way from what it had been.

The Shining One looks upon this and Yo-El, and smiles.

"May I?"

The Shining One gives His approval, and Yo-El turns to send out his presence, his call to be one.

Several of his brethren pause and look this way and that but, not seeing Yo-El, they return to their … whatever it is they are doing.

"*They are trying to answer the calls, just as you have done with your brethren, and they have done with you.*"

"Can these Callers not hear them?"

"*Not at the moment.*"

The Shining One sees that Yo-El is at a place in his being where it is time to return. So He becomes very complete with him and in the next moment of consciousness they are returned to their very same place as they have come from.

All in the grouping wish to rush to them, but the Shining One tells them to not do so at this point. He calls to the fore his brethren and Yo-El and the Caller, and He begins to emit light, or ... energy seems to begin to gently move from Him to the center of their group, their form. Then His brethren follow and do the same.

Yo-El and the Caller soon realize that he is calling the Father.

The Father is there, and they hold their form in honor.

The Father tells Yo-El and the Caller,

You have learned much (and there is more) of my gifts that can express themselves in many different ways. And they're there for you to choose when you are ready.

Yo-El understands and the Caller looks at him and accepts that Yo-El understands.

The Father blesses them all and they know that they can release their form.

All of us rush forward to embrace the Father, and oh, isn't it so beautiful! Oh, we pull the Father into us and He pulls us into Him. We are reminded of the great, undulating waves of light, and we feel those and we love it so.

The Father tells us many things and we all ask Him about these things that He shares with us and we find great joy in them, and we have many experiences with our sweet Father in His all.

Then, it is time and we give our love to all here, for the Father has gone to His special Place. We give our blessings of love and our personal light and energy to all here, and we move off, out of the All ... soaring, rotating about, giving out our love and our light to all, all about.

Many experiences pass, and Yo-El leads us to the Heaven Place. We can feel that some of our grouping are hesitant to come to the Heaven Place and then they look within themselves and they find great joy in going to it. We find great cheer in the discoveries that we have gathered from all of these creations and the understanding that the Caller has given us and shown unto us.

There are many more of the Shining One's companions, the brethren of the Shining One. We are in wonder of their number here in the Heaven Place, and, as we are observing them, we see them ... one here, two there, gently moving through the elements.

"What do they do?" we ask Yo-El.

Yo-El calls us to be one and gives that to us, and then we understand, and he communicates with the brethren, and we all gather together. He asks, "What about our group ... those of our grouping that have gone into the No-Place? Have they answered any calls?"

The Shining One's brother shakes his head, "No."

We look upon him in wonder! "You have taken one of those forms that they have created."

He smiles and nods his head-thing and we find great cheer in this, and then others come, too, and we look upon them with wonder. "These are beautiful forms," we tell them. "Do you give up your freedom to have this?"

The first brother smiles at us with his head-thing and then instantly becomes the light of his true being, and we find great cheer in this and we laugh and become one and roll about in our joy at this wonder.

Many things come to pass, many experiences.

Then they sayeth to us, "Will you journey to the No-Place?"

We look at Yo-El, and he answers, "Yes."

"Do you wish us to teach you these forms?"

Yo-El answers, "Yes," and many in our grouping begin to rattle and clatter with their colors and light and energy, and so we all find great humor in this.

"What is it? You do not wish to know how to be these form-things?"

Then they realize that it is that they fear that they shall lose their freedom ... the beauty of their creation and their oneness with the Father.

Yo-El sayeth nothing but turns and the brethren respond as though he had spoken to them.

"Come here. Join with us and we will become one with you and show you these things."

So we do and we find such joy in being one with them because their energy and light is so beautiful. It feels so much as though it is the Shining One.

After, we have been one with them for a number of experiences and now we know many things. So we come into oneness with Yo-El and ask him, "Can we move off?"

So we do and he gives his love and his light to the brethren of the Shining One. We move easily and swiftly to the beautiful presence of Consciousness, and we become ourselves in our uniqueness. We communicate many things, and some say that they do not wish to experience the definition and move into the No-Place because, "Look, our brethren have gone into the No-Place and they did not take these definitions, these forms, and still they have not returned. If we take these forms, what will come of us?"

The Caller, Il-Em, and Yo-El come to the center.

Yo-El sayeth to Il-Em, "Tell them how you came to answer our call back to you."

Il-Em begins to tell them how he held the memory of his being and his brethren and the Father way deep within him, in a place within him that the others could not know, for had they known it, they might seek to cause him to give that away to some other thing.

Many of us do not understand this.

So he sayeth to them again, "It is not that they have that right nor that … you might call it (this word) *power*, over us, but it is something that they use, their consciousness, in groupings, to convince … to get the consciousness of many of our brethren to join in oneness with what they sayeth. It is of that sort of nature. Some … and I will tell you this in the spirit of truth within me … Some gather together and, in a manner of speaking, cover over the consciousness within one or several until they are not knowing that consciousness any longer, and, so doing, they become theirs. And this is that thing that you were told of in an experience before now."

Many of us move away a bit and sort of move off, that we can drift with this and take it into our uniqueness to see if we can keep it within us and still be that beautiful expression as the Father has given it to us.

Some have a very strong reaction and cast it off, and begin to do strange things. We come to know this, that they are bringing their uniqueness from its truth and purity within to sort of pass all through their expression. Several of these move far off and sort of hover there.

We find that these curious terms and expressions that are used in the No-Place are coming more and more into our consciousness, into our oneness, and we understand that this is that thing called knowledge. So, we make a place within ourselves to put these things that they will not move all throughout our being and sort of clutter it up. We wish to keep our beauty and our wonder, as given by God, very pure. Now here and there several others move off … not gone, but a distance away.

Il-Em turns to Yo-El and states, "It is as I told you, my brother. It is very difficult for those who have not been in the No-Place to hold even the consciousness of it, for the consciousness has a … I will call it quality, as if it were a life unto itself, that the knowing of it seems to gradually move all throughout one's expression, until everywhere you look there it is. And those who are now moving into a position to … I can hardly speak it … make others theirs, they are using these things. So …" and he looks about to those who have moved off, "they know this, of course, and they do not wish to experience anymore of it."

Yo-El nods and affirms this and very gently sayeth, "Of course. And they are righteous in their being, and so it is that they can remain in the beautiful breath of God, His grace, His love, that they can claim these and remain. We could try to explain to them and show them that it is always here," and he points to touch Il-Em in the midst of his being, "but the light of God is, as well. But we both know that they will not choose it and that is their right."

We move about to gather those who are still with us and then we move to come into oneness that we can go to our brethren who have moved off and give them our love. It is such a beautiful exchange. We love them so.

As we do this, we remember (as we love them) how much we love our brethren who are now in the No-Place, and the knowing of them pulls upon us and exceptionally so, Yo-El. We can see the light within him, very near to where God is, growing.

After many experiences we move from them, keeping the line of that wondrous thing, that wondrous consciousness-thing of light between us, and we look upon it with love and with fondness. It moves about with the light of our Father as we have chosen it to be a living connection to these, our brethren, who remain behind, who we love so dearly.

We discuss, now in the Heaven Place, as Yo-El intends

to strive to make the Symbol again, that some of us can move in that spirit form to know our brethren there in the No-Place.

So the brethren of the Shining One quickly come to make the positions and the Symbol is made, and it begins to glow and pulse and become very beautiful.

Il-Em, Yo-El, and the Sister move up together and they become one in their completeness.

We look upon them as they move into the No-Place. For a time, we ponder why we did not make those lines, those light-line things, but then we know that Yo-El knoweth these things. So we claim the peace of God and the Symbol is maintained, with the glowing lights where Il-Em, Yo-El, and the Sister had been.

They move very close to where that special breath of God-thing is, and they are there ... and it is beautiful.

The Sister, AoLe'A, leads them to where the brethren are.

Yo-El sayeth to Her, "Can you tell if they can hear us? Can you tell if any have answered who have called?"

In their completeness, She becomes something most exquisite, and Il-Em and Yo-El marvel at this beautiful, exquisite expression that is now separating from them.

Then, it is a shivering sphere, beautiful, crystalline ... and moving. To their wonder and awe, She is still with them.

The crystalline sphere moves, and we know that this sphere is of God.

"Yo-El," Il-Em asks, "What is this that She does?"

The Sister, AoLe'A, answers, to his wonder and joy, "I am yet with you."

We laugh at this ... gently, for we still are concerned we might disturb them.

"I am sending that which is my right to be with them. It is that which I intend and it is that which is a further expression of this, our spirits."

They want to ask more but they do not. They merely observe.

Then, the shimmering sphere comes back. Suddenly, it is within their completeness and it is over the Sister for a time and becomes one with Her.

They begin to move, and instantly they are back in the Heaven Place. Slowly, they settle down to take a previous position, and in a curious, beautiful way, they become one with themselves.

Some of us on the periphery find humor in this. Then we move into our uniqueness here in the Heaven Place and we gather about to share this experience that this Sister has gathered for us.

She sayeth to us, "Pause a moment and find that Place within you where the Father is, but do not call Him."

So we do. It is a glorious consciousness.

We hear Her speaking to us, as though She were inside all of us. She sayeth to us, "Here is that which you seek to know."

There is a sudden rush, a flurry of energies and colors and sounds and lights and so much more that we feel that we are being filled to overflowing.

Then She sayeth a thing and we know that we are naught. She tells us to put this in our Knowledge Place, and so we do.

They say a wonderful thing to God together and they release the Symbol and she moves off to be with the brethren of the Shining One.

We give Her our love and we give to Her a line of light, if she wishes it, and she takes them all.

We find this so wonderful that we become one and move out of the Heaven Place so that we can sing and dance to the glory of this. We send so much light and energy out into the Consciousness that our brethren who had left come to be close by us and we give this to them, as much as they wish. Some take quite a bit and put it in their Knowledge Place; others take only a small part and move off again, and we give them our love, for we understand.

Then we come into our uniqueness and Il-Em speaks to us. "It appears that they are in the No-Place. They do not know us. They do not hear us. They have taken up positions with those who call. If they could not reach the Callers, then it is clear that we now cannot reach them."

This causes waves of differing energies and colors and lights to pass all through us.

Yo-El tells us, "Just see that. Don't take it within. Let it pass from you." So we do.

We share much and we discuss much.

Then Yo-El tells them that he shall go into the No-Place.

Many of us sayeth to him, "Perhaps they shall come in a time, as they measure that, in an experience ahead? What will you do there?"

He sayeth to us softly, "Am-El, the Shining One, has told me that if one comes to show them, to teach them as He taught I and my brother here, that perhaps they can find their way if they move into their spirit."

Many of us try to gather about him, asking him to become one with us again that we can become complete and move, that we can go out into the Father's colors and go to the Word of the Father as it unfolds the magnificence of His thought, His spirit, His being, all these things which we have come to know.

128

But we know immediately, for we are with him and shall ever be, that there is that light in him next to the God Place that shines brightly. We look to Il-Em and he has the shining Place. To our delight and surprise, Il-Em comes to us to point to the center of *our* being and we see that we have the shining Places, but ours do not shine with the light and brilliance and energy of theirs.

We choose to have lines-of-light with them as they move back to the Heaven Place, and many of the brethren of the Shining One, Am-El, are encircling them and moving with them, parting the elements.

And they are gone from us.

We feel a strange thing and we see our colors. What is happening to our ...? We try to become one, but we cannot bring forth the harmony. That thing comes and some want to take it, to hold onto it, because they feel they are losing something. Perhaps this thing will make them more complete, this weeping-thing.

Suddenly the light in our midst rises and we are overjoyed to see Am-El!

He gathers our surrounding in oneness and many of His brethren come from the All and surround us to give us their love and their light, and we feel our completeness surging back to life. We look at one another and see the beauty of our uniqueness.

Am-El sayeth unto us so sweetly, *"You know not yet what you have created with these lines-of-light. You are now feeling what they are experiencing, and this is one of the powerful expressions that they have created in the No-Place. It is coming to you along the lines-of-light, which is your living expression. Now you must learn to be the master of your own uniqueness, your own beauty, and now I will show you how you may do this:*

"Much has been born into awareness, in Consciousness. It has expression in Consciousness insofar as one chooses to know it there.

"But it is not of a life of its own in Consciousness; it is only that which they have called, Knowing.

"The beauty of each soul bears forth something so beautiful and so exquisite. That, as one comes to know this in the uniqueness of each of our brethren, we quickly know and are, indeed, brought into magnificent beauty, as we behold that there is no other just like this one, which is the brother or sister of God, as God has given it to them."

8

Not Eternal

Many experiences have followed and in the midst of these is the intent of Yo-El and Il-Em as they encounter the experiences being shared by the Shining One's brethren, and they are questioning that they might the better know how those works have progressed in what is called the No-Place.

As they experience the expression of a form they discover within themselves that it is, indeed, a work of beauty. Yet there seems to be the intent to define and limit. Insofar as this is, indeed, unknown to them save for their journeys into the No-Place, even Il-Em ponders how far they have progressed in defining and creating uniqueness in the form of separation.

They call together as many as are willing and they begin the movement through the elements to find where the brethren are unto whom the Sister, AoLe'A, has communed.

As they come unto them there is the pause, as Yo-El ventures forth alone to reach out to them. He seeks that special Place within him where the Father is with him in completeness, but he does not call the Father forth as his brother, the Shining One, has shown him.

It is the light of his going unto the Sacred Place that is first perceived by his brethren in this element. Some are very startled by it. Others seem to be in a state of greater and greater peacefulness as they approach the light being radiated by Yo-El from the Sacred Place within.

They come, and Yo-El thinks now might there be that commune with them. So he reaches out with an intent to do so, and their approach slows and they turn and move back to join their grouping.

Yo-El ponders this, and as he does Il-Em approaches and they become one. Yo-El embraces him and Il-Em embraces Yo-El, and in their oneness they begin to perceive from the Sacred Place within. As they do this their combined light reaches out again.

This time, many of their brethren pause in their works to turn and look. Some move forward with considerable swiftness until they are being touched by the fingers of light.

One of them looks this way, and that and after a brief pause we can see him summoning his consciousness, his true being. As he does, the light around him begins to grow, and in that moment Yo-El reaches out to him and grasps him with love.

The brother responds in a moment with some unsurety, thinking it might be some of those of the brethren who are in the No-Place. But he feels the light from Yo-El and Il-Em reflecting within him, and his own light begins to grow and grow.

Now several of the others in the element realize and begin to turn and come unto the light, as well. And as they do, the light grows and grows.

Suddenly the Shining One's brethren are surrounding them, preserving them, in a manner of speaking, that the light can grow without disruption.

The Shining One's brethren guide them to the Heaven Place. Here, they allow the uniqueness of each of their brethren that they had previously surrounded to come unto their being, their individual being.

Those of us here wish to rush to our brethren and embrace them and become one with them, but we receive a caution from Yo-El and several of the Shining One's brethren. So we merely stay in our consciousness in oneness, and hold for them our love.

There is much embracing and Yo-El and Il-Em are

asking them, "What have you discovered?" and of course, it is difficult for the brethren who have been awakened to come from the element to stop being joyful.

We move closer as we see their joy, and Yo-El turns to look upon us with a bit of laughter and beckons us, as he realizes that the brethren who were lost in the element are now, unto their uniqueness, complete.

We rush to them and embrace them and we do the dance of celebration and the laughter and joy, and we move all about into Consciousness and into the All as we seek to show everyone, all our brethren, that these brothers and sisters who were absent from us are now returned!

We become one, all of us. Even the Shining One's brethren join us, and we call the Father and the Father comes into our being.

He sayeth unto these, our brethren,
"Have you had a good journey?"

Some of us find this to be joyful and humorous, for it is only they who have had a good journey; we have longed for their presence.

The Father turns to us as we find this joy within and touches us and embraces us in a special way, so that we know His love realizes what we feel and supports it.

Yo-El goes unto the Father and asks, "Have I been appropriate here, Father?"

He looks to the brethren who are returned and asks them,
"Would you answer for him?"

They rush to Yo-El and embrace him mightily. "You have indeed. You have reminded us of our oneness with the Father, and that we are not of the No-Place but of the Father and His Word.

There are many experiences and sharings.

Then the Father embraces us in a oneness, and then we

are one and the Father has departed from us in that form. But the presence of Him is in that Sacred Place within, and glowing.

We move about and laugh as we soar among the colors of the Father's Word, giving the Father's life from the Sacred Place unto the colors. As we do this, they seem to burst into greater color and radiance, and dance among each other, giving to one this and to the other that, and more beautiful colors are born as the result.

There comes a point in our experience where Yo-El asks of us, "Would you journey with me to the Guardian?"
We say, "Of course."

So we are instantly with the Guardian.
He looks upon us with a great smile and sayeth unto the lost brethren who are now found, "Welcome. I am glad to be with you in this way. But thou knoweth I was ever with you, yes?"
They look at one another and realize they hadn't remembered this.
So the Guardian goes to each one and, in a certain way, makes his presence in the Sacred Place.
We look upon this with wonder and then we become one, that we can see that his presence is in *our* Sacred Place.
We resume our uniqueness and ask of him, "Brother, how is it that they did not have your presence?"
He turns to us to say, "It is not so as you say. I merely have awakened my presence within them. It was ever there."

We look upon each other and we begin to understand, and we find great joy in this.

Realizing our intent, the Guardian steps back with a great smile, and we collide with our brethren who now have the Guardian in their Sacred Place again.

We roll about through consciousness, inviting others of our brethren as we encounter them, and so the celebration goes.

Finally, we journey to the All and we embrace all of these, our brethren, and the Shining One.

He comes to Yo-El and Il-Em, placing His presence within them, and He gives to them something that we cannot see. But we can feel it. It is a blessing of the nature that the Father gives, and we love it dearly.

"What is it that you are intending now, my brother, who has become teacher?"

Yo-El laughs mightily. "I do not believe that I am, as yet, that which you call teacher. I wish to learn the nature of what our brethren have discovered and why our other brethren continue to remain in that element."

The brethren who have come forth to be (in our terms) *free*, come to the forefront, and one comes forward to speak for them. "We had studied the elements and explored the nature of these, each one. When we came upon the one that we came to *rest in* (in a manner of speaking), we thought it to be the last one, that we could sustain our uniqueness and still explore the nature of being in the No-Place. They are creating many, many structures, and in these structures they are building other definitions."

"Of what are these structures?" questions Yo-El.

Il-Em looks down and moves this way and that.

Yo-El notes this and asks him, "What is it that you are feeling?"

Il-Em moves over to E-Am, who is the spokesperson for the rescued ones and states, "Is it as I am experiencing?" and he becomes one with E-Am a

E-Am answers, "Yes. It has progressed much beyond this."

"Share it then," Il-Em states.

E-Am gathers himself, and several of his brethren come to be in oneness with him that they can support him in the sharing of it. "They are creating a structure of *be-ing*. And the structure of being has progressed into varying groupings into which they have formed to support their intent. They have fashioned unique qualities that are a part of the structure.

"These qualities define, even greater, the nature of their consciousness as they move about in the No-Place. The beauty of the No-Place grows as we perceive it, but many of our brethren who are in the No-Place are losing their consciousness of the beauty."

Yo-El turns to the Shining One and asks, "How is this possible?"

The Shining One merely smiles and gives him love, and asks E-Am to continue.

"It is a progression that (they call it) that they have defined. The forms that you have been shown by the brethren are now in a different manner of structure; they create the forms themselves by coming together and building. In a manner of speaking, they have devised that which builds a structure within a structure, and this is called form. The form now seems to be separate from the All ... from Consciousness. I tell you this ... hold it, surround it with love: It is, in many respects, separate from *God*."

"Why do they call the Father this?"

"It is because," E-Am responds, "they have lost the memory, for the most part. So they call the Father this because they think of Him as something far distant."

"What is the form that creates the form within it or ... as you stated? Tell us more."

"They have created patterns, and in the patterns they build these definitions, and the definitions in the patterns give the patterns strength. As I found from being one with you, you saw with the Shining One in your journey how they had taken these small portions of the Father's light and used these to give ..." and he turns to his brethren for a moment and turns back to continue, "they give what they call life to the structures, the creations they love."

They all are puzzled, those who come with Yo-El and Il-Em, and even though the Shining One calls His brethren to surround the grouping.

Yo-El calls them to become one, and he calls E-Am and his to be with them. In their oneness, understanding is built. As the experience unfolds, they come back into the beautiful peace and sweet joy of oneness with the Father. "Thank you, E-Am, and all of you dear brethren, for this gift. It is quite ... How shall I call it my brother?" turning to the Shining One.

The Shining One looks at Yo-El with a smile and states quite succinctly, *"Interesting."*

We all find great humor in this for it is, indeed, quite *interesting.* We find this expression to be quite delightful and we go about to greet one another and say to them, "You are very interesting," and we find great humor in doing this.

As that experience passes, we return to Yo-El and Il-Em, who are much amused at our joy. "We are here to help you, all of you, to reach our brethren. Perhaps, if we can reach our other brethren, we can decide ... you know, choose."

We pause for a time to absorb these communications and many others that come with them.

Finally, Il-Em asks E-Am, "How do you come by these

energies, these *definitions*, as you call them? Are they from the No-Place?"

E-Am nods, and the others as well. "It is quite, in a manner of speaking, magnificent. They have used so much of what the Father has given them to create this and, as you could call it in their terms, it has of its own nature grown or, as they call it, *evolved*. And in the evolving, it has taken on even different forms. It is truly wondrous to behold, and in a manner it speaks to you … it calls to you."

"Show us," asks Yo-El.

They become one so that E-Am and the others can share this knowledge with them.

They feel it and touch it in their oneness, and Yo-El turns to the Shining One, "I think we should call the Father." Yo-El looks carefully at the Shining One, for He is becoming very bright and very beautifully illuminated and we see humor in this.

"You already have," He comments.

The Father comes with a brilliant light and it cascades all over us. We celebrate it with a great joy and in the joy of celebration do we find that more light comes, and more.

Finally, we move off into Consciousness as the Father guides us, and we share this beautiful light the Father has given us with all of our brethren, and the Father sends it forth upon His Word.

"What is this beautiful light You have given us?" Yo-El asks gently.

"It is the greater understanding of who you are and the potential that is yours as my gifts to you."

"Do we not, ever, know who we are, Father? We are Your Children."

It is so, the Father answers with sweetness.
But look within yourself now and see what I have given you."

So we all do, and we see the beautiful light and we feel the energies of the Father's Word. And a wonderful thing occurs. Our uniqueness and the Father's light begin to do a wonderful thing. It is likened unto the individual colors and their beauty and how they dance together. Within us is something like this beauty, and it is rather like a dance within.

We laugh and share with one another the beautiful light within each of us, and when all of us have known each other's beautiful lights and the, as the Father tells us, the harmonics of these, we begin to understand the nature of this gift.

> *It is rather, my Children, that I have called it forth within you and awakened it. As you have called forth the light from within your brethren, from the element, and brought them here to what you call Home, these are the potentials that you have within you, as well as without.*

> *It is not only that you are my Children, but you are that which is Eternal.*

One asks the Father, "What is this that You sayeth to us?"

The Father smiles and looks at E-Am and his followers, and E-Am nods. "It is as I have given to you," he replies. "It is that creation, that structure, they have builded. It is, in a manner of speaking, so defined and structured, beautiful in its nature, but it does not have, as the Father has just said unto us: It is not eternal,"

At first we cannot comprehend this, and then we look within to where they have given us this gift of their oneness with us. And we find it.

Some of us do not want to bring it forth, and the Father touches them gently and shows them that they are complete and in oneness with Him, ever. So, with a bit of

140

gentle humor, they pull it forth and look upon it, and we pause for a time with the Father as we feel the meaning of these things.

> Then it comes that the Father sayeth unto us,
> *I shall move now, that you can explore these new, (as you call them) gifts,* and He smiles to us all.
> *And when you will, I am with you.*
> *Know this:* and He looks upon each of us and calls forth the Sacred Place within each of us, and holds it up.
> *See yourselves, here.*

He takes it unto Himself, and we are in wonder and awe as He then brings it forth again and, with one motion, gives it to each of us.

We look within, and the light of the Father is more brilliant than ever before!

> *Be ever, then, my Children, in joy of our oneness.*

And we perceive the Father no more.

We journey off into oneness into the colors, for it seems the colors ever give unto us great blessings and awaken within us a sort of vibrancy, like E-Am calls, *renewal* and that thing they have created of birth.

So we celebrate in the colors. We are one with them, and we experience in a peaceful state.

Many experiences follow.

Some of our grouping journey this way and that.

Others decide to join Yo-El and Il-Em and E-Am and the others who journeyed with us from the element, back unto the Heaven Place.

The Shining One and those with Him tell us that they shall be in the All but they are with us, as the Father is with us. We look within and see the lines-of-light connecting them and we laugh with good joy over this.

This time the movement into the Heaven Place is different. As the Shining One's brethren who are here welcome us, we give unto them all that the Father has *called forth* (as He calls it) and they celebrate with us for a time.

Yo-El, E-Am, Il-Em and a number of us pause and we look about at the elements. We create the sacred form that the Shining One has shown to us.

We all leave our positions to move into the center of these sacred forms, and we journey and we soar through the elements with complete ease. We come to the last element, where we find our brethren. Some of them look up with a start and look about. Others are very focused upon whatever it is that they are about.

But we do not linger here. We move on, and come to the beautiful Place where the Father's Word is and we bask in this. We are in wonder over its presence, and we feel the Father's love and His peace. And we look back to the elements above, and the No-Place below, and we see the magnificence, indeed, as E-Am and his brethren have showed us.

We soar down into the No-Place. Here and there some of our brethren need to become one to a greater degree. So we reach within and find those gifts of the Father, and call them into being. Our peace and joy are complete again, and as we soar back through the
No-Place we see many things.

E-Am and his colleagues point these out to us, and we pause to look upon some forms giving forth new forms from their own being. Some are so delicate and they seem to soar, as we soar, in the Consciousness of the Father's Word.

We gather more awareness and we move away again, passing into the great River of Light that is our Father's love, and we give our love to the Father and we feel Him embracing us.

We move towards the Heaven Place and we realize, in greater depth and breadth, the nature of the structure of the elements and all that is about them. We come unto the place where others of our brethren are doing their work and we look upon this with curiosity.

E-Am comes forward. "It is what they do when they are seeking to build understanding. It is called a work. It is, in truth, a focus of their attention."

Yo-El asks, "What is this *attention*-thing?"

E-Am and his brethren laugh and they say, "If I put a point of light right here before us all," and he does so, "look upon that point of light and nothing else."

Some of us are startled, because how can you be one and not know all things?

E-Am comments to them, "Try and do this as I sayeth to you. Remember how you look at a single beautiful color? Think of looking at this beautiful, little sphere I have created and that alone."

We try to do this, and we feel ourselves creating strange energies.

E-Am calls this *working*.

We laugh at this because it feels so very strange. But we manage to *attention* this little spot for a time.

Then the little spot scurries back to E-Am, and we find humor in this.

"This is what they call *work*, in the No-Place, and this is what we strive to do here in this element, that we can, through their means, understand … and find pathways to speak to them."

We can all feel the energies changing just a bit, so we move swiftly away from the element and soar past all else into consciousness of our Father's Word. In the sweet Word we feel like we can, curiously, be our own uniqueness again. In this we find humor. We also find curious discoveries, and we discuss this.

E-Am states, "It is that way in the No-Place. Their uniqueness is kept within and, to an extent, rarely comes forth now. Most of them keep their uniqueness to themselves. Some of them gather in groupings and strive to make those who have kept their uniqueness within unto this pattern or unto this structure that the grouping has cleaved unto."

We ask him what this means.

He states simply, "They choose it." Then he reminds us again as he has shared with us.

So it unfolds for quite a time, as they measure it in the Earth.

Then we determine that this creates a strange reaction in the beauty and uniqueness of our being. It seems to slow the beauty of our being in a curious way.

E-Ude comes forward and asks of Yo-El, "Is this work-thing trying to come here into the Father's Word?"

We all become one again that we can share in the completeness of this oneness, and we go within to find the Sacred Place.

As we do, the Father is immediately present and we ask of Him, "Is it possible, Father, that we could bring this work-thing to Your Word?" We do not know how to ask this of the Father.

But the Father understands and sayeth to us,
You can bring what you wish here, but my Word is always my Word, and the consciousness of it that you know is ever and always of me.

We find great joy in this and we ask the Father more questions in regard to these things and we give them names from E-Am.

E-Ude comes to ask us, "Can we feel these again from you, E-Am?"

So we do, and we strengthen our uniqueness as we do this and now we understand them so much better.

Many experiences follow and we explore and seek to understand much of what they have given us.

Then there comes that experience, or as they call it, point of *time* ... for they measure in a curious way, and we have found that they use these to give understanding and definition, for they have lost their ability, or forgotten it, to become one.

Yo-El asks of the Shining One, "I wish to learn, my Brother, what is the nature of the Sacred Symbol that You gave to us?"

E-Am comes forward, as does E-Ude and Il-Em, to sit very closely near the Shining One.

We feel the Father radiating from Him, and He tells us softly, *"All these things can be known to you. You have only but to go within yourselves and find these in the harmonics of the beauty that is your uniqueness."*

He gives us the understanding of these communications, and as we draw upon E-Am's teachings and those from Il-Em, we are coming into understanding.

"All of that which they have created," E-Am begins, "is based upon form and the form they have drawn from the Father's light. It is this that they use to give expression to their form."

We ponder this for a great time and finally come into the realization of it.

"In the Father's light," begins Yo-El softly, "there is

that, then, such as the Sacred Symbol you have given us."

The Shining One merely nods to him, His love for Yo-El shinning brightly as we can see it

Yo-El reciprocates this to Him. "Can You give to me this or must I find it?"

"I can give it to you," the Shining One states, *"but not in a manner that I would take one of those little spheres that brother E-Am created ..."* (and we all find great humor in this) *"but in that I can call it forth for you from within your very being."*

"Will You call it forth then?" and Yo-El moves over to be one with E-Am, and reaches out to embrace E-Ude and Il-Em, and they come into a state of being that is wondrous to behold.

The colors of the Father's Word are dancing all about upon them, and now they call us to be one with them that we might know this as well, for all is shared here but when we are ready, that is all that is required. We marvel at this, the discovery of the utter beauty of the Father's Word.

So we soar with all of us together, to the colors and, with this awareness, we look upon the colors in a new way and we *see* them! Each is unique and creates a resonant reaction to the others nearby. We take a portion of a color and bring it over to some of the other colors and immediately there is a resonance of form, and the form begins in beautiful sound and vibrations that seem to tingle all the parts of our being, all at the same time, and we laugh as we find that which the Father has gifted us, or awakened within us, is responding to these harmonics.

Then we feel more resonance coming from elsewhere and other harmonics singing out that are, as they call it in the No-Place, a great distance away and we pause to feel and know this in the completeness of our beings. We strengthen our oneness, and we build understanding and we surround ourselves with understanding. We realize in this manner so have we embraced the No-Place in what they call a time past, and that became the Heaven Place.

Now we take and create the Heaven Place in a manner of ... same nature around us here and we are delighted with it, and the colors seem to be, in a manner, enjoying it as well, for they sing and dance together all the more.

These experiences grow and become many other experiences and we begin to understand the magnificence and beauty of the Father's Word in wondrous new depth and breadth of understanding.

Some in our grouping say they wish to journey far, far into the depths of this *understanding* (through the nomenclature of the Earth ... which we are finding is quite convenient at times). So we use it here and we define to one another these things that are ... how do we understand it ... a part of the expression of the Father.

We ask the Shining One, "Do they know of this?"

"They are striving to understand it again, but they do not know of it. They know that they can use the Father's light in certain ways, and some of the colors and energies. But they do not understand why or what the gift is; they merely use them."

"Will they be ... ever ... set free?" E-Ude asks.

Now the Shining One rises up that we can all perceive Him with clarity and singularity. *"This is a part of their structure. They are free."*

"What?" questions E-Ude.

"I say to you again, they are free."

We share with E-Ude this wonder. "How is it possible that they are free? When we engage them they seem like they have lost the life of our Father's Word."

The Shining One sayeth, *"That is a part of what is their creation, that they have manifested to seem as such."*

Yo-El comes forward and states with joy unto the Shining One, "I understand, my Brother! It is the Sacred

Symbol that You have given to us that grants us access to the forms, the structure, that we can be there and pass through these without disturbing them. So can I conclude from this that we could engage the forms and know the life of the forms?"

The Shining One smiles and nods in approval to Yo-El. *"But bear in mind, my brother, it is their right, their choice to have created the structures, just as much as E-Am has created the little sphere for you to see."*

"Let me know this more profoundly," Yo-El comments slowly.

They become one and then, very swiftly, Yo-El moves into his uniqueness. And in wonder he sayeth to us, "I understand. Shall I give the understanding of this to you all?"

Some say, as they look upon Yo-El and see it and feel it that they do not wish to have it just yet, and there is humor here.

Others of us come to Yo-El in our love for him and our oneness for him and Il-Em.

E-Ude comes, representing us, and sayeth, "We wish, we brethren here, wish to know this and share this with you and the Shining One and all the Shining One's brethren."

In that, there is a wonderful transformation! We find ourselves in the No-Place just as simply as choosing it! We did not pass through the elements, to our knowledge; neither did we make any action. We simply are in the No-Place.

Then Yo-El takes the knowledge, and we are back in the midst of the colors! We are in wonder of this!

The Shining One sayeth to us, *"This is only a part of the*

beauty of the Father's Word. Remember, that which you find in the No-Place is of their choice. It cannot be taken from them, lest you are grievance unto yourself for having done so. You do not wish this. Even though you seek your oneness with your brethren and wish to give them gifts, they must choose it."

We ponder this for a great experience. We move out into the Consciousness of the Father's Word, and in the vast beauty of it we look at all these things.

Yo-El and his brethren say to us, "We are now to return to the All."

And they are gone.

We discuss these things and which actions shall we do that we might seek oneness with our sweet brethren whom we long for. So we come into oneness and, in the Sacred Place, we call the Father, and the Father is here.

I see you have gained much of the color and energies and gifts that I have given.

"How do you see this?" E-Am asks. "Dear Father, how do you see this?"

I see it because it is I all about you and within you.

"Oh Father, that is so wonderful,"

The Father turns to Yo-El and, in a curious and beautiful way, reaches into Yo-El and, then, returns to the center of our grouping and sayeth to us,

I have placed the truth within your brother. If he wishes, you may have it. I have placed it within him because he has asked and has chosen to do a thing.

We all look at Yo-El, for we had not seen this, but the Father clearly did.

The Father sayeth to us,
*I shall move now, that you can share and make
your choices. I am with you, ever.*
And the Father is going back into the Sacred
Places.

So we gather around Yo-El.
Il-Em looks carefully at him, and we see through Il-Em
what he sees and we realize that our brother will go into the
structure, in the No-Place, honor their choices and seek to
keep that gift from the Father, that they might know of it,
and choose not to destroy ... not to take from them, but to
tell them of their freedom.

9

Being the Peace

Many experiences are had as we move about exploring and experiencing the wondrous gifts the Father has pointed to within us. Of particular delight is the experience of moving within and under and above the particles that come from within the Word as they burst forth to comprise the various colors. It is as though each of these stimulates some part within us, and we feel the joy and laughter come from each one as they pass through the sparkling fount of the Father's Word.

More experiences are had, filled with the joy of our Oneness, and we journey to be with our sweet Brother, the Shining One, and His colleagues. Yo-El asks of Him to consider his thought, his love within, and so they become one. We observe with wonder and equal joy. We feel this radiating from them, and we understand as we feel it. Then, they separate into their uniqueness and others of the Shining One's grouping come to embrace them.

As we join with them in this embrace we hear, *"It is possible for you to do as you are seeking. And as long as you are paying heed to that which has been given to you, and to be guided by those who have come from the grouping in the element, then I should see that you should be aright in your quest, your journey."*

E-Am comes forward and states, "I should be honored to join you and equally so E-Ude and, of course, Il-Em."

The Shining One contemplates them, each one, and they feel and respond to his loving exploration and we feel this too. Then He smiles and states, *"One of my brethren comes forward and states he would offer his spirit and his light to your quest, if you would accept."*

Yo-El turns to greet this one and with a great smile and a burst of expression of love they embrace one another and become one. As they separate, after a time, we all come together in oneness that we can feel as each of them have felt and know in oneness this journey that lies ahead.

We move instantly through the Symbol to the Heaven Place and, as we arrive, many of the Shining One's brethren have gathered to greet us. It is clear that they know in their oneness of our arrival and our intent.

"I leave you now, my brother, to the good presence of my brethren here, and Lom-Sa who has requested to join you." He embraces his brother and departs.

Lom-Sa is greeted heartily and with great joy by his brethren here. As we move with him and Yo-El and the others, we see clearly that Lom-Sa is dearly loved, not only as each is loved, but for the beautiful spirit that shines from him. Not the same as the Shining One, different in a sort, but equally beautiful. We can see clearly that his love for our Father and his choice, as it might be called, have given to him great energies that are given to us all. But he takes these and brings them into the completeness of his uniqueness and from here, deep within in the Sacred Place, they shine forth.

Some of our brethren have come to state that it is their choice to journey back to the colors and the movement of the Father's Word; that they would find greater joy in pursuing these gifts; and that they, with the line-of-light, are with us ever. So we give them our good graces and our love, as we have learned to do in the journeys we have taken.

The decision is made to move into a closer proximity to the No-Place, so we become one through the power of the Sacred Symbol and move. As we are near to the element from which E-Am and his brethren have come, we pause and there is the commentary that is as follows ...

"Do you seek to use their form or do you seek to move without form?"

"I should think," responds Yo-El, "that it would better to move from the Sacred Symbol without form. And perhaps you," pointing to E-Am, "and, of course, the others can guide me into understanding where they are in their current movement of their, as you have called it, structures or such."

There is a ripple of humor here, for the amusement is that we cannot comprehend as yet the intents and purposes for these. So it is rather an odd thing for us to be discussing when we know it not in the fullness of consciousness.

One in our grouping asks, "Why do we not know it through the Father?" and laughter fills the grouping.

As we express this laughter, some in the element from which E-Am came turn, look this way and that, and go back to their focus.

It is our brother Lom-Sa who has come to the forefront and answers, "We can. We can do this. We need not be here to do this nor go into the Earth (as it is called by these, our brethren) to know it."

"Interesting," responds Yo-El. "Which would you say is the better, my brother?"

Lom-Sa moves and becomes in oneness with Yo-El Momentarily they move to their uniqueness, and he, with loving smile, states to Yo-El, "It is to your choice that you journey there. For in the experiencing of it, in the manner that you are holding within you, you will grasp in the better sense of a knowing than to just simply know it."

"How does this differ?" one in our grouping asks.

Lom-Sa turns and states, "It is different because Yo-El is different, and you are different as are we all. It is that difference that makes us treasures unto the Father and to each other."

The questioner laughs with loving understanding.

"Then shall we move to the Father?" questions Lom-Sa of Yo-El.

"I think it would be wise."

We are somewhat curious that he answers this, for it seemed he was about to embark into the No-Place.

We strengthen our oneness and we come into that state from whence we call forth the Father, and His joy and embrace is welcomed.

It is true, the Father responds softly.
You can know all that you seek, for we are one with they. But what you seek is the experiencing of it. Is it not so?

Yo-El curiously studies himself.

We find this delightful, for, as he does, we see the lights and colors and energies of his uniqueness coming forth from him. We feel these and they are like being one with him.

"Is it true Father," Yo-El begins softly "that knowing and experiencing each have gifts to give?"

That is true, my son, as you have come to know ... as all of you have come to know. But you need not engage, what you call, the No-Place. You can know what you seek, and experience it here in this oneness.

The Father looks upon Yo-El with tenderness and understanding, waiting for Yo-El to make the discovery that the Father knows he shall.

We feel this from the Father and we are very, very still so as not to disturb them.

"I see in the knowing with you Father, as some of the others apparently have already seen, there is a time that comes wherein there will be *challenges*, as they call it; where the uniqueness of the individual will be ..."

We see him pausing to understand enough to express it here in the energies of our commune.

It is true, the Father interjects
But you need not quest for it, for I can give it to you

to a degree, as you would find it appropriate. And by
this I mean, I cannot go to that Place within you and
call forth what lies ahead in their, as they call it,
measurement of time. For, if I so do I would, indeed,
usurp the beauty of the gifts I have given them. And I
would not do this thing.

I tell you that you are righteous in what you seek,
and that if you continue, and those with you, I know
that you shall not err.

But mind this very carefully again: You must honor
them as I am honoring them now by not giving to you
what lies ahead in their choices and journeys. And as
you do this and remember me in that Sacred Place
within you, you know, do you not … All shall be of
goodness and be well in the heart and spirit of you and
all those you encounter. It is your choice, my blessed son.

He pauses, and we find in this a wondrous thing, for he
is beginning to radiate, as does the Shining One. It is as
though the Father is giving to him some special, beautiful
love. As we know this, the Father turns and gives it to us, as
well. It is so beautiful. We go within ourselves that we
might be one with it in our uniqueness. Then we bring it
forth and give it to each other and into oneness in a
beautiful collage of the Father's great gift to us.

As we now move back into our uniqueness we see
Yo-El smiling brightly. "Thank you for calling this forth, my
Father. I shall bear it, ever, as I know my brethren here
shall do the same."

Very well then, sayeth the Father.

With a final touch to all of us, the Father
moves into His Special Place.

"Let us move, then, with gentleness and ease in the
Sacred Symbol's power and in our oneness." So sayeth
Lom-Sa.

As we pass through the final element, we see the magnificence of the Father's Word flowing. We rush into it and laugh with great delight and glee as we feel it seeming to bring us into being all over again. Then, after passage of some experiences, we move towards the edge led by Yo-El and the others. As we come into that which is the expression of the No-Place, we pause in wonder.

Some say unto Yo-El, unto Lom-Sa, and the others, "Look, it is as though they have taken of the Father's light! See how it dances as the colors dance, but only just so far," and we feel that thing pulling at us. But we strengthen our oneness and resume our joy.

E-Am moves to the forefront beside the others, and we move with gentleness to engage in the energies of the No-Place. These are separate from that of the colors but they have the feeling of the colors. They do not dance or sing as they do in the Father's Word, yet we find them beautiful, and we give them our love and they love us in return.

We move to the No-Place, and many of us feel a sort of curious jolting. We look to E-Am and he comes to each of us and gives to us his consciousness, that we know of this. Then we move a bit further, and we see some of our brethren! We so want to be in oneness with them. They look like they are not complete.

E-Am gathers us to explain. "It is, as has been explained earlier. Do you remember the focus, the being attentive to a thing? Many of these are truly focusing upon those things that they are about."

Some of us ask, "Why are they about these things? We do not perceive them?" Some in our grouping find a bit of humor in this and others encourage them not to express laughter here.

So, we continue to move, observing our brethren and many others who are not a part of our grouping but whom we know clearly as our brethren. Again, the feeling of wanting to share our oneness with them surges to the forefront, and we are calmed quickly and easily, for we are in oneness.

"What are these?" Yo-El points to several ... we shall call them *things* for the moment.

E-Am states, "They are creations."

We look upon one another and ask, "Did the Father place these here?"

"To our understanding, yes, to a degree, insofar as all is of the Father. But it has been by their choice and their oneness with the Father, and they have continued on in the shaping and the forming, as has been shared earlier that the structures are becoming manyfold. Look you here and see the uniqueness of many of these."

We move to an area where there are many things all in a close proximity to one another, and suddenly the things begin to move off very swiftly. So we follow them with ease and see them twist and turn as they move this way and that. Then we are shown others ... so many, and so many have such beauty in their simplicity but the uniqueness of their creation is not complete. It is as though a part of the beauty of the Father has been *withheld*, in a manner of speaking.

"What is this?" we ask of E-Am.

E-Am states softly, "To the best of our knowledge, it is because they wish to ... possess them."

Before we can ask, E-Am gathers us together into his consciousness and shows us this, and we see other such experiences, and again and again different ... some very strong, others as though they are just beginning, and some seem to be chosen by others. And some other curious energies are arising out of this.

Lom-Sa tells us softly, "Do you not think, Yo-El and the rest of you, that we have gathered enough knowing for the present?"

We concur, and we move with graceful ease immediately to the Heaven Place. We marvel, yet, at the wonder of this movement! It feels as though we are moving with the Father's Word. It is so delightful.

It is curious, as we encounter the brethren of the Shining One. They have gathered together, and, with them, is the Shining One and many of our brethren who had moved off. We come together and we settle ourselves as a grouping focused upon whatever it is that the Shining One has to give us.

Yo-El moves to the forefront, as do Lom-Sa and the others. "What have you concluded my brother?" he asks of Yo-El.

"I have many of these, I believe they call them, *forms* or *energies* that are my realizations from journeying in their midst. It is curious, for they seem intent to (and there is quite a pause) ... They seem intent to further their separateness."

The Shining One merely nods an understanding to Yo-El, and Lom-Sa comes beside them both, as do E-Ude and E-Am.

We hear them, and we move so that we can be one with them.

"If this progresses as it appears, then I can know, clearly, what it is that our Father has said that He would not reveal without disturbing their right of choice."

E-Am states, "We have seen some of these beginnings. But, as I stated previously, they are moving in what they call rapid time ... swiftly. The measure of it is not by our knowing. It is by their perception of the movement of the No-Place, which, again, they have called Earth."

"This movement, then, is how they gauge? What do they gauge?"

E-Am and Lom-Sa look very carefully at one another.

"They gauge," E-Am continues "their existence, and

the existence of those things which are of their intent."

We all look at one another, and we realize through the knowing that the existence is a movement from what the Father has stated is our gift, our Eternal Self. "How is this possible?" we ask, not intending to interrupt but we are one with them, so it is permitted (with a note of great joy here), and we are received with joyful laughter.

"It is, again, their intent, their choices and the structures and *creations*, as they call it, which are merely just as many of us have done with the colors and then never had an intent to make them ours or take from them their beauty of expression."

"How is it that they make the colors to be …"

Lom-Sa interjects, "Without vibrancy, without *life*, as they call it?"

"Do they not realize or remember that these are merely creations?" questions E-Ude?

"Well, you see and experience and know as you have. That is what we know."

The Shining One calls for us to move out of the Heaven Place into a state of oneness, and in this oneness, the Shining One calls for us to bring forth our uniqueness that we might give this to bring a great joy and brilliance of our light and to celebrate and dance and sing.

So we do with great gladness.

Then, after these experiences, the Shining One sayeth to us, *"Let us call our Father."*

We do, and the Father is immediately before us. He moves, looking at each of us, smiling, touching us, and giving to us His love, His peace, His understanding of those things we have discovered and do not understand. After He has passed unto all of us He moves to the center of our grouping. We give to the Father our love and our great joy and we thank Him for this gift as He has given it to us.

One in our grouping asks, "What is this gift You have given to us Father? We know it and You have given it to us often and we know that it is within us. When we see the things in the No-Place ... Oh, they call it *Earth*, Father. In the Earth-Place these things seem to, in a way, take a bit of that from us. No, no ... not so. Rather, it seems to strangely cover over Your gift."

The Father laughs with us as He brings an embrace to the one who is questioning, and sayeth to him,

> *Well done my son, you speak well. It is, as you say, curious.*
>
> *What I give to you is always yours and the experiencing, as you say, of the things, of the No-Place (also called Earth) is the call of them.*

"The *call*, Father?"

> *Yes, it is a part of their intent. And when you hear their call placed in the things, you accept these as you accept oneness with each other.*
>
> *But they have chosen a pathway that is different from the path or paths that you are following, my Children.*

One of us wants to ask why, but we have learned from the past that it is their right. So she does not ask this and we all smile at her and even the Father, for we all are One and we know this.

> *It is good that you remember, my sweet Children, that these are your brethren and that they are, as you, on journeys to explore and to build a knowing.*

One says to the Father, "Well, why do they not come here and know with us? We would like to know with them." Again, there is laughter.

> *Perhaps in a time they will do so. But you could know with them, if you wish to.*

That one who asks looks to each of us, and then smiles and says, "No, I think not. I don't want them to cover up Your gift."

We find great humor in this, for the Father has told us this gift is ever with us, and that all we need to do is reach within the Sacred Place and bring it forth.

And greater than this, my Children … You have only but to be it."

We look at one another and we look to see who is *being* it and who is not *being* it.

The Father smiles broadly,

No, that is not my meaning. It is when you face these things, when you feel their call, that you be my gift, and you can experience the things and not let them cover my gifts.

"Have the others let their gifts be covered, Father?"

The Father pauses a moment and answers,

For a time, it is so.

Have you any other questions?

"Oh Father," comments Yo-El, "I feel my love for our brethren, all of them, but especially so those with whom we have journeyed and celebrated. We feel in our being a place where we wish them to be again, and we wish to give to them, but they will not receive from us."

The Father studies Yo-El carefully and then looks to the Shining One, who smiles gently and nods in a curious way.

There are many experiences that they are seeking. Some of these experiences are not to your understanding, and perhaps in a time they shall be, or nay. But it is yet as beautiful as your choice to go and dance among the colors of my Word, for they to have intentions to create the structures and the things and to take of my gifts to them, as you might take of them and direct them as they would.

But, ever, if you keep this as you have questioned,
which you may call my Peace, it is that which is always
going to bring you into understanding and into that
state where you and I can move into oneness with great
ease, as we are now, here.

The Father embraces us all, and finally turns to the
grouping of Yo-El and the Shining One and all those with
them, and looks at them with a love and smiles, and they
know that the Father gives to them their right of choice, as
He has given it to us all.

Remember ever, my Children, that I love you.
And the Father is gone to the Sacred Place.

"How can I go to the No-Place," begins Yo-El softly
"and speak to my brethren within the structure?"

The Shining One looks carefully at Yo-El, *"I have a*
knowing, my brother, that there shall come a time when I and
many with me shall answer a great call that shall come from the
No-Place. I have not received that call. Therefore, if it is your
wish to journey there, I give to you Lom-Sa, my dear colleague, to
be your guardian, as can be any of the others who would so
choose."

In a brilliant light, Il-Em comes forward and states,
"May it be my honor to so do. For I have been called and
therefore, perhaps, I have a line of light that can be used by
my brother Yo-El."

"So is it then," the Shining One responds, *"and the others*
of you can be a part of this as it is of your call, your wish. But I
cannot in the direct sense, for it is not my, as they call it, time. Go
on to my brethren in the Heaven Place, my sweet brother. And my
brethren who are journeying with you … They shall guide you as
to the pathway, and you may choose at any time, any point in the
experience to return here, and wait."

We feel this, curiously, as new energies from the
Shining One.

Lom-Sa moves to briefly be one with the Shining One, and we hear them and we feel them, but we do not clearly understand. But we have no matter over this, for we are seeking the special gifts of our Father that we may bring them to the forefront, that none of these things or the intent of them, the discussion of them will, as they say it, stick to us.

We move with our brethren to the Heaven Place, and we feel something that passes all through us. We bring the Father's gift to the forefront and *be* it, as the Father told us, and in the being of the Father's gift there is, as He has named it ... this great Peace.

So now we move with ease. But we can see the thing. It is most curious. It is like it is moving back and forth beneath the Heaven Place, not strong but a sort of wispy thing that we know is from the No-Place. "What is this?" we ask of E-Am.

"It is the movement of their structure, I believe, and it appears that their structure grows and grows and has developed some uniqueness until itself."

"Uniqueness? Like the Father's gift to each of us?"

"No, not in that way. Of a similar nature, but not in the sense as you ask. It is not of the Father, it is of our brethren and their making."

A grouping in our midst goes over to Yo-El and asks him, "Yo-El, sweet brother, we feel something. We do not know this thing, but we do not feel joy in it, nor is there laughter."

Lom-Sa comes to our grouping and states, "It is so, as you have discerned it, and that is well done. But perhaps you should encourage each other to surround yourselves with the Father's gift. We are together in this intent, and we will preserve our sweet brother Yo-El."

10

The Giving Gift

A number of experiences have transpired here and much sharing, and they come to a point in the present where Yo-El looks upon the vastness of the expanse before them. Observing once again, the energies moving and swirling, he turns to Lam-Sa and asks, "Are these those created forces of the Father that they are directing here?"

Lom-Sa turns to E-Am and they commune for a time. "We do not know precisely, Yo-El, but it appears that they are not of a singular intent. By that we mean, they do not seem to have a singled out purpose. They are, apparently, simply in motion."

Some of the Shining One's brethren suggest to them that they form the Sacred Symbol and journey forth a bit to explore these, and in the knowing of them will come the greater understanding of other experiences that lie ahead. So they do.

From the beautiful Oneness there is this experience of such a completeness. Yo-El and all the others bind themselves in the love for the Father, and the journey commences.

At first there is no reaction on the part of the forces, the energies that are swirling.

Then Yo-El states very gently, "Let us commune with them."

The others agree. Some little laughter comes from several of our brethren, for the question comes forth without being expressed, "How can you commune with these? They have no uniqueness."

Nonetheless, Yo-El reaches out.

Immediately, the energies stop their motion and gather about his expression.

Very gently Yo-El expresses the Father's love to them, and there is a burst of light filled with colors, and all in the

Oneness are smitten with awe at the beauty.

E-Ude states very softly, "Not outside of the beautiful colors of the Father's Word have I seen such magnificence. It is truly an expression of our Father here,"

Yo-El nods and turns to Lom-Sa and asks softly, "What is it that we are to do with these?"

Lom-Sa, studying carefully the colors that are gathered around Yo-El, "I would say to you, my brother, that there is no need of doing. They know now that we come in our Father's Name. Look you here, all about the beauty that has grown from our communing with these colors. It is as though they seek to give all that the Father's Word births unto Consciousness."

"Yet," Yo-El comments, "here they are. Should we not seek to free them?"

Lom-Sa comments softly, "Know thou not my brother that they *are* free. There is naught that can truly be confined lest the Father permits it to be so, and through the will and choices of our brethren. So do we encounter this here. Perhaps it is something that they are intending. I would suggest that we journey to the last element and see if we cannot commune now with some of our brethren ... those whom you have been journeying with and who are observing."

This brings a ripple of joy all throughout our grouping, and we look to E-Am.

He states, "Indeed."

So we do, and we are immediately here. We find that the element seems to have grown and become something that is very peaceful. We look at one another again and do not comment, but merely share our wonder at the growth and beauty that is here. It is clear that it is still stationary but it is like being in one of the Father's colors that is at rest.

E-Am is the first to reach out to commune with those

of his brothers who are here in the element, and some of the sisters, as well.

It is one of these sisters who first turns away from that which was her focus to look this way and that. Then she awakens the Sacred Place and we feel her and know her. Oh, we are so joyful, and we call to her, "It is we, your brethren!" The joy spills all over our grouping, only, with the caution that is coming to us from Yo-El that we are to give Nov'A a bit of opportunity to balance.

We realize as we look into her being that she has gathered much beautiful information and much knowledge in that Place, so we bide ourselves, and look at one another with great joy and humor until she comes unto us. We sweep her into our midst, and the laughter and joy passes all throughout each of us.

Then comes the passage of experiences that she shares with us, and we are in true wonder of these. We ask her, "Nov'A, what is the nature of the rest of the grouping here? Are they still aware of their oneness with us? Do they not seek oneness as in past?"

Nov'A smiles with her beautiful light and turns to Yo-El and states very gently, "We are yet one. But we made the choice to become, as they say, a part of those things that we are observing, that in that way we could know these. Let me return to my brethren and touch them, that they will remember the Sacred Place," and without another commune, she moves unto the brethren.

Oh, it is so beautiful to see her light!

When they are touched by it, it seems to pass all through them and it is like they are re-awakened unto our oneness. Some do that shaking thing a bit. Then, they perceive us, and they come and we celebrate with them.

Nov'A continues until she has reached the very last one who, at first, turns back to observe in the manner that was being studied, and Nov'A touches him again and he comes.

It is Yo-El who states, "I think it well that we move, *now*."

So we do, and we are instantly in the beautiful Heaven Place, and there is such celebration that even the Shining One's brethren come and join our oneness.

We move off in to the Word of the Father, turning about and celebrating, singing great songs and dancing, and all those of our brethren who are in the Word of the Father hear our song and celebrate with us.

Finally, we come unto a place where Yo-El and Lam-Sa join together and say unto us, "Let us become one and celebrate with the Father, and ask of Him what we have done."

E-Ude questions him, "What do you mean by *what we have done*? We have gathered up our brethren."

Lom-Sa touches E-Ude, and immediately he understands that it is that we have done a thing in the spaces, the elements, of the No-Place, and we wish to hear from the Father that this has been a good thing to do.

The joy comes echoing off the Oneness as we seek the Sacred Place, and in this calling cometh the Father.

The Father's smile upon us is like being renewed in a sense of realizing so much through the gifts of His giving and the wonder of His beauty. It passes all throughout our grouping, and Nov'A begins to sparkle with the Father's light. The Father goes to her and embraces her.

As He touches her we hear Him say,
I am of such, a joy to be with you in this way again, my Child.

"Oh Father," she says, "it is not that I have not known You ..."

I know, He responds before she can finish her words. They become one and we know, as they know, that the Father sayeth to her,

In the sweetness of your effort, have you given. And in the giving there is such a beauty that comes forth from the gifts I have given unto you.

I wish to say unto you of my love and joy for that which you have gained and claimed of my gifts.

We are in wonder over this gift ... the Giving-gift. As we look upon it we search within ourselves, and find that it is there also among the gifts the Father has given to all of us. But Nov'A has called it forth, and in a wondrous way it has become of her being, of her uniqueness. So it is the gift to all of us to share this with her.

A number of experiences pass.

The Father pauses and looks upon us all and states,

It is good that you have done this. You have done well, and you have not violated any right of their choice. You see, it was the choice of your brethren that they could answer you ... or nay. And since it was their choice to answer, here we are, together in this way, celebrating.

After some experiences of joy, Yo-El and Lom-Sa ask the Father, "We thank You, Father, for this wondrous gift that You have given to us all. And now we ask of You, is it still well, what we intend?"

The Father knoweth this from within them.

He sayeth to them,

Be in my gift of peace and all shall be well. Remember: I am ever with you.

And the Father goeth to the Sacred Place.

We commune with one another, somewhat in wonder, for we had anticipated that the Father would give us something. Then we begin to laugh, for we know that the Father within is all that we shall ever need.

We return to the Heaven Place and share in our uniqueness with all of the Shining One's brethren, and then comes the end of this experience.

We pause to look upon the No-Place, and now we see through the wisdom of our brethren who have been observing and who have gained the understanding of much that is transpiring among our brethren.

Yo-El and E-Am speak to Nov'A and she answers, "It is, indeed, wondrous what they have created, and from the knowledge that my brethren and I have given, you can see what we have observed."

E-Ude questions Nov'A, "Why do they create this death-thing?"

Nov'A smiles upon him and states softly, "It was quite interesting. They came to the agreement, rather in oneness but in a different way. They have taken their oneness to a level in the No-Place that resonates with the finite definition there, and in a manner similar to our oneness do they share through the communing, through their forms, and through their consciousness in the finite sense."

"This is most interesting," comments Yo-El, looking at Lom-Sa, who nods somewhat serenely, for he is, as we can perceive, knowing the information that our brethren from the element have given us. We honor this experience of his knowing. We give it, what they call, time.

"It is, indeed, beautiful ... the structure and breadth and depth of how they have fashioned their definitions and their structure," Lom-Sa begins softly, "and we cannot know until we experience it, what its reaction will be to us. Do you all concur that it is good for us to know this now?"

We all look upon Yo-El and we see him touch the

Sacred Place, and the light grows around him and he answers, "I think it so. Let us journey."

As some in our grouping begin to form the sacred Symbol, Yo-El sayeth to them, "I shall not journey in the Sacred Symbol. I wish to know this in the manner that they know it."

We look at one another, and we realize his intent. We feel it from him. So we agree that we shall journey in the Sacred Symbol and surround him with our light and the Father's gift of peace.

Yo-El agrees, and so we begin.

It is curious at first because, wherein in past there was little reaction found (the other elements and the energies as we move through them), now there is a sort of rippling effect where their colors react to our passing with Yo-El in our midst. But they do not become that rigid-thing. They remain supple, and so we pass through these.

As we come to the element of our brethren, we look upon the beautiful No-Place Earth and we see the colors they have woven into it and the energies of our Father's Word. It is truly beautiful, yet the longing for oneness with our brethren, in particular, those of our grouping whom we have known and loved so intimately, calls to us.

Yo-El turns to us and touches his Sacred Place, and we find peace, as does he.

The movement through the beautiful Word of the Father that obviously He has placed here is exhilarating for us. We pause but for a brief experience, for Yo-El's intent and choice become empowered by it.

We move, yet surrounding him, and we engage the structure and the Elements here that have been fashioned into definition. We look upon them. While we can feel them, we observe Yo-El who is moreso knowing them, and we see the uniqueness of his being change as he encounters these. We look upon the surface of the No-Place Earth and we see that the colors they have woven into structure are very beautiful. There is a calling within us that wants to dance among them as we would in the Father's Word, but Lom-Sa embraces us with a caution and the Father's peace, and we place that longing within us in the Knowing Place.

We now engage the surface of the No-Place Earth and we see Yo-El knowing it, and we hear him striving to commune with the surface ... and only a gentle response. Yes, it is glowing with the Father's Word, but so softly.

We commune with Yo-El and he tells us that they have chosen it to be so. We look upon one another with wonder and we contemplate why we would have it so, and we go to our Knowing Place and remember that this was to be a gift to the Father. So we claim the Father's gift of peace.

Yo-El begins to move and we with him, and he turns to us with a warm commune saying, "Be at peace, my brethren. I find naught here that is not of the Father."

In the wonder of it, Yo-El leaves our midst and moves upon the surface of the No-Place, soaring gently above it, encountering the creations of structure and communing with them, and finding the beauty of the Father in each.

He passes over a vast area that calls to us all. And Yo-El moves into it! Lom-Sa calls to us to be at peace and have no concern.

We perceive Yo-El moving within it and coming to a pause, and we see the vastness of this creation shimmer the Father's colors, and even radiating out to us. We feel its beauty and we feel the gifts of the Father in it and we are in true wonder of this! How have they created this? Clearly the Father's hand has rested here and given life to their intent.

Yo-El emerges from this vastness and looks upon us

with joy, and enters our midst again to share with us the knowing of it. We are bedazzled with the magnificence of this gift from the Father. It is like being one with the Father, here in the No-Place!

Yo-El sayeth, "They call this the water-thing. Clearly it is a part of the Father that continually loves this No-Place Earth. Somehow they have ..." He pauses, and we feel what he feels and know what he knows, and we all touch the Sacred Place for a moment. In the Father's peace-thing Yo-El continues, "The Father has contributed this to perpetuate, in a manner, their creations. It is of such magnificence!"

We move slowly, with Yo-El yet in our midst sharing with us, and we come to a place where the No-Place Earth is different, as it was when we first encountered it. We look upon the differences, and the grouping of Nov'A gives to us the knowledge that they have and we place this in our Knowledge Places.

Yo-El blesses us with the Father's gift and moves forward unto the No-Place Earth again. He soars ever so softly across the surface, feeling and communing with all of the structures.

They respond to him gently, and we so love this. It is like talking to a small part of the Father's Word, and we keep our oneness in the Sacred Symbol, that we do not disturb them. Oh, the energies and beautiful colors of the Father awaken within us.

As we see Yo-El approach some of the brethren, we become very, very still.

Yo-El moves ever so gently to be in the midst of a grouping of them.

None appear to know him. Some turn to, as they call it, look upon him (in their forms). One studies him a bit, for Yo-El has not the same as they do ... a form, and that one turns at a moment and goes back to what their grouping was about.

We can feel through Yo-El that they are doing one of
their work-things. We see that they are taking from the
creations of the No-Place Earth and making of them, and
we feel a bit of a pull as we see them take some of their
creations and change them.

There is a movement as Lom-Sa gives to us the peace
of our Father's gift, and we are well.

We feel their communications with one another
through the wonder of our observations, given to us by
Nov'A's grouping. She comes to the forefront and sayeth to
us, "Would that I might journey with Yo-El."

We look upon one another with wonder and we wish to
commune with Yo-El but, curiously, he is changing his
uniqueness, so we cannot reach him.

Nov'A sayeth to Lom-Sa, and Lom-Sa gives to her a gift
from his Sacred Place, and she leaves our grouping.

She moves slowly so as not to disrupt that which Yo-El
is doing. But Yo-El can feel her presence and turns to look
upon her and gives to her his love, and she reciprocates this
to him.

Somehow, Yo-El is doing something to the beauty of
his uniqueness, and once again he moves to the grouping
before him and moves into the midst of it.

This time, several in the grouping stop their work-thing
and look about, and Yo-El continues to change his
uniqueness.

To our wonder, he reaches out, ever so gently, toward
one of them! We are very quiet.

Nov'A is moving about the periphery, encircling them.
As we see her do this, we see some of the Father's gentle,
vibrant colors being embedded by her.

We ask of Lom-Sa and E-Am, "Is she creating one of
those things? Is she creating a structure?"

E-Am shakes his head-thing with a smile (as he, too,

has adopted, somewhat, the expression of those of the brethren whom Nov'A is encircling).

Without commune, E-Am moves from our grouping, and from the knowing he has given us, we understand that he knows somewhat of this nature, and now he is striving to express it.

Nov'A goes to him and envelops him with her light, and they become one. Nov'A and E-Am return to our midst, and we become one with them.

Nov'A sayeth, "It is not good for you to do this thing."

E-Am sayeth to her, "I wish to help Yo-El."

And Nov'A sayeth, "He has not asked of you to do this thing," and we find great humor in this.

So E-Am receives her blessing and extends to her some of the gratitude-thing, and Nov'A departs again with a smile. (We love her light and her warmth!) And she returns to the grouping and continues what looks like a sacred dance around the grouping.

We ask of Lom-Sa, "Does Nov'A dance within their right of choice?"

Lom-Sa pauses and goes into his Knowing Place and touches his Sacred Place. And the light of the Father comes forth and sayeth to us, through Lom-Sa, *All is well. It is a good thing.*

We become very quiet again and move very close, and we hear Yo-El offer himself in commune to the one who has obviously felt his presence.

With wonder, we see this one move closer to Yo-El, and with swiftness, this one summons his brethren, and they swirl about Yo-El until we cannot see them ... nor Nov'A!

Lom-Sa gives to us, with great power, the Father's gift, and we find the peace again. "Be of good cheer," Lom-Sa sayeth. "Yo-El is in his peace-thing. They cannot do as they are intending."

Nov'A is still encircling them all and we understand that because she doeth this sacred dance around them, they cannot summon the others to come and join them to do their capturing-thing to Yo-El.

After many passages of their time, we see them separate, and we see Yo-El in the center, yet in his beauty and in his uniqueness. We see the grouping resting their body-things, and we feel their intent was as we have in the Knowing Place.

Nov'A no longer encircles the grouping but goes directly to Yo-El and surrounds him with her light, and we feel something. It is like when we first passed through some of the elements, the first Element. It is a foreboding. We do not understand this so we go to our Knowing Places and find it from the grouping of E-Am and Nov'A. They bring forth peace and understanding.

Slowly, Nov'A, surrounding Yo-El with her light, moves towards our grouping, and, after a pause, moves within our grouping. We look upon them with wonder. Yet Nov'A surrounds Yo-El with her light, and Yo-El is quiet.

Lom-Sa sayeth to us, "Let us return now to the Sacred Symbol."

Immediately we are in the Heaven Place and the brethren of the Shining One come into oneness with us.

With gentleness, Nov'A rises up, surrounded by our grouping and oneness, and moves off into the Word of the Father.

We look upon Yo-El and we reach out to him, but Nov'A sayeth, "Do not, for he is yet recovering his uniqueness and knowing it."

E-Ude comes forward and sayeth, "What is it with my brother? Has he been ..." and he pauses, seeking from his Knowing Place, "*influenced* by our brethren of the No-Place

Earth?"

Nov'A does not respond but continues to embrace him.

To our wonder, we hear her sing a song, and immediately, our sister AoLe'A is present. We are in wonder and joy of Her beauty and light and uniqueness.

She moves ever so sweetly to embrace Nov'A, who is embracing Yo-El, and very swiftly they become one. We yearn to become one with them, but AoLe'A's light tells us do not do this thing.

So, Lom-Sa sayeth to us, "Let us dance and sing songs around them. This will bring joy and wonder to the light that AoLe'A is giving," and so we gladly do this. Many of our brethren come, having heard our song, and join the dance with us, and they look with wonder upon AoLe'A's beautiful light and give to Her their love, and She accepts it.

After some dancing, AoLe'A brings Her light into Herself and we look … for there are Nov'A and Yo-El shining in their beautiful uniqueness that we so love.

AoLe'A sayeth to us, "What you have known here is a part of that which lies ahead: Those of you who seek to journey to the No-Place Earth must know that it is their domain, and their structures and choices have, as they call it, power. While this power cannot, as you can see, *do* anything to our brother Yo-El, if you seek to know it at the level of their expression, it does cause your uniqueness to go within you, and they would do that thing to make you a part of their structure."

We are in wonder over this. We go to our brother Yo-El and he welcomes us and we become one with him, and we become one in the sacredness of our Father's Holy Place, and it is good.

And the Father comes.

We surround him with our love.

Then, after some experiences, He looks upon AoLe'A and embraces Her and She, He.

She gives us her love and departs to return to the Shining One and the All.

We look upon the Father who is embracing Nov'A and Yo-El.

He sayeth to us,
It is good that you have been quiet in the No-Place Earth, for it honors their choices to do so. And you, my so, Yo-El … You have now the knowing of it in your uniqueness.

Yo-El states, "I do, Father. I know it."

Then He turns to Nov'A and sayeth to her ever so sweetly,
You are my beautiful daughter and you have taken of my light to embrace this, your brother. And this is a beautiful work that you have done.

Nov'A goes to the Father, and they are one.

We see the beauty of His love for her and they both give this love to all of us, and we find great joy in it.

After some experiences the Father sayeth to us,
Be about your joy for a time and know this as Yo-El and Nov'A know it, and remember: I am ever with you.

And the Father goeth to His Special Place.

We look upon our brother and sister and we feel the wonder of them! They have gone into the No-Place and have known it!

Those who dwelled in the element and E-Am move to them to give them what is called a Gift of Blessing. They accept it, and the Gift of Blessing is given to all of us and we accept it.

Now, Yo-El cometh to us in his uniqueness and sayeth, "Let me share to you those things that I now know and I

179

have experienced to that level of fullness, that you would choose."

We look upon one another. *What is it that our brother sayeth to us?* So we ask it of him.

He sayeth, "It is curious, for the knowing of it has imparted something within me in the Knowing Place, and it is quite unique. I have not, as they say, come into understanding of it completely. I offer it to you with the knowing of that as I have just said."

We look upon him in wonder and at each other, for we have not known such as our brother Yo-El sayeth to us.

After a time, E-Ude sayeth to us, "Why do we not go to the colors and be one in them and let them rain upon us their beauty within and without, and then we shall decide."

We all know this to be good.

So we come into oneness and immediately journey to the colors of our Father's Word, and it is as though they knew we were coming. They greet us with bursts of wondrous vibrancy! The (as we have known them) small particles of the various colors come and do a dance within us and we laugh and sing songs and celebrate.

Many experiences are shared.

Then it is Yo-El and Nov'A who come into expression of their uniqueness and sayeth to us, "We would journey to the Guardian to seek from him a knowing."

We all agree that we will journey to this brother Guardian, for we know him to be good and he gives to us beautiful gifts from the Father.

As we come upon our brother, the Guardian, we pause and see that his light is so much brighter, and we are in wonder over this. Rivulets of light come and dance among us and we look upon this and laugh. It feels so exhilarating.

Then, Lom-Sa sayeth, "Let us be at quiet-thing and listen."

The Guardian sayeth in sweet communications to us, "There is much ahead, dear brethren, and I wish to give to you my gratitude for the gift you have given."

We look upon one another in wonder at this!

And to our surprise, Yo-El leaveth our grouping, moves directly to the Guardian and moves into his light, and embraces him. Swiftly, Nov'A follows and doeth the same. Then, the others go to the Guardian, and so we doeth the same.

In the embrace of the Guardian we feel the wonder of the light he has gathered, and he sayeth to us, "There is much that is in the growth-thing... much that is coming to you in the Knowledge Place. Be of good cheer and, as you would, open yourselves to receive it."

So we do.

11

In the Sacred Symbol

Much has transpired, in terms of experiences, and there is, what could be called, a time of discussion and reflection. Many of us are with Yo-El and those of the others and we hear them discussing with the Guardian various of their experiences in the No-Place Earth and also receiving comments on teachings from the Guardian who knoweth much, as we all attest here.

In the midst of this communication do we find this of interest from the Guardian: "There are those you know in the No-Place Earth who you cannot hear calling and, yet, if you go within to that Sacred Place and call out from there, you shall find that there is a call in a different manner. For the call originates within them and, thus, you would only hear it within you in that Sacred Place."

We all look at one another with wonder.

Yo-El and Nov'A and several of the others move closer to the Guardian, that they can exchange his communications in oneness. As they do, we listen and share with them as we claim oneness with they, as well.

The Guardian explains carefully, that Yo-El and Nov'A and all the others can understand them, that "The challenges that are presently in motion, in other words growing in the Earth, as there is that quest for dominance, the quest for control of various things that we do not have knowledge of."

We look upon one another in wonder and our thought is, "Why would they do this?" So we put this in the Knowing Place to think about, as they have taught us, and we listen to the closure.

Yo-El sayeth to him, "Then, could we come into oneness, our grouping, and hear this call?"

The Guardian studies them carefully, as though he is looking into the Sacred Places within them, and we look at one another and smile, moving closer, that he would look into our Sacred Places. So he does, with a gesture of love.

We find it most exhilarating, for he has the light of our Father, and the colors come from it.

Now Yo-El and Nov'A move off into the Word of our Father, having embraced the Guardian, as have we, and we begin to experience.

E-Am and the others in his grouping sayeth, "It might be well for us to move to the Heaven Place, that from there we might hear these calls, as the Guardian has said it."

So we do. We are greeted, of course, as always, by the Shining One's brethren, whose beauty, we think, grows with each meeting. We approach them, with bright laughter and a celebration of oneness, we think, to dance and sing songs.

But E-Am sayeth to us, "Better it would be that we would be about what Yo-El and the others are seeking to know."

So we honor this. We call the guardians together into the Sacred Symbol and we join them. This time, as we form the Sacred Symbol, many of us gather on the points, that we, too, can be a part of this movement. And so it is.

In our movement, those of us who have not journeyed in this manner but only known of this through the oneness and the line-of-light, we find this to be most exhilarating. But as we pass through the elements, we pause our exhilaration to be quiet, for we see the elements and we remember these. It seems that for some reason they do not wish our presence. We shall put this in the Place of Memory, that we can do the thinking on it later.

We continue to move and we pass through the element where our brethren were, E-Am and the others and Nov'A, and we pause here and become one, that we can give this with our love and our gratitude for their good service here.

So we leave our light and our laughter here, and we

move on.

It is most interesting (we truly love this word) ... It is most interesting for us to experience the movement in the Sacred Symbol. It is as though we are a part of everything that is about us, even though it doesn't seem to want to be a part of us.

As we continue to move, we encounter the beautiful River of Light that we know to be the Father. We cherish this time and illuminate ourselves all throughout as we feel the Father's light passing through every part of us, renewing us, and restoring the beauty of His gifts to us, that they shine within with brilliance.

Now, Yo-El sayeth to us, "Let us draw together in our oneness and move beyond, into the outer expressions of the No-Place. Be alert now and we shall seek to hear the calls that the Guardian sayeth are within."

So we move (as they measure it) a distance into their No-Place. We feel the wonder of their creations, and we marvel at how beautiful some of the *works* (as they call them) are. The nature of these are, indeed, living, with the vibrancy of our brethren, to such a degree that it causes us to long for them and to wish that we could be one with them to share what they have discovered and give to them the gifts that we have awakened within us.

We all form into the Oneness of expression from where we would call the Father, but we do not call Him (as Yo-El instructs us to do), and an interesting experience unfolds. Nov'A moves to the center and begins to turn about. As she does, we feel an awakening occur within us. We hold this for a moment of cherished awareness, and then she moves back to the circle of our oneness. And Cel'A, a sister of our grouping, moves to the center and turns around and about, and, again, we feel this curiously beautiful awakening within. Then, finally, she moves back and is one with us, and we are very quiet, in the quiet-thing way.

At first, we cannot hear but a curious vibration of movement within the Sacred Place ... but off over here where it is in the area of our memory of our brethren who have journeyed to Earth. We are in wonder of this! We look upon it and surround it with our love and the more we do this, the more it seems to be energized, some curious way, like the particles of light when we dance among the colors. It grows and grows, and, with great wonder and awe, we look upon this in the center of our grouping as we are in oneness.

There, before us, is the image of the brethren! We are so joyful to see him again, but we caution each other as we are in oneness, to be in the quiet-thing.

We hear, to our wonder, "Greetings, brethren."

We look upon one another, "Who sayeth this?" We look to the center and it is he, our brother! We want to ask him, "Where are you? Are you within us?" and we are back into the quiet-thing, for we know Yo-El will question him ... or that is our hope.

To our surprise, it is Nov'A and two of the other of our sisters who go close to him, and we ponder this for a bit. Then we go to the Knowing part of our being and find the reference here to how Nov'A surrounded Yo-El and helped preserve him from others who might seek to dominate. But we wonder, "Who is here to dominate? It is only we, who love him," and we receive a glance from Lom-Sa and know to do the quiet-thing very, very well.

It seems that our sisters are moving about him in a sort of slow movement of dancing love, and we are wondering more and more, for we are experiencing this in our Sacred Place within the Oneness. My, how beautiful are the gifts our Father has given to us! We continue the experience of observing until we hear ...

"Thank you for answering my call to you." Shem-El moves just slightly, that his communication will be close to this, our brother.

We hear, "You are Shem, are you not?"

We feel the love pour from him, and we watch closely as a tiny ribbon of light seems to become apparent between them, just very dim at first, and sort of wandering about between them. Now it grows, and in our oneness with Shem-El, we can feel that it is he, Shem, who was a part of one of the groupings who went to the No-Place Earth long ago. "How is it possible that you are able to do this?" we ponder, and we hope that Yo-El will recognize our questions and he does.

Yo-El asks of him, "Shem, my brother, speak to us of how you have done this, what you are doing."

We hear him say to us, "I am a distance, by their measure, away from where you were. I knew you were present but I could not call back to you, for they would have known that I was still your brother."

We are in wonder of this! How could he ever not be our brother?

Yo-El turns to cast us a loving glance and we remember to do the quiet-thing again.

"Let us come to you," Yo-El states.

The maidens are stationary now as Yo-El moves very close, but not beyond the boundary of the maidens.

"Very well, I will you tell you, here, how you can find me."

The ribbon of light between them grows very bright and some movement of light goes back and forth between them, but, curiously, we do not know this in our oneness. But we stay in the quiet-thing.

"So shall it be, then," Yo-El states, and he moves back into the circle of light that is our oneness within the Sacred Symbol.

The maidens begin their movement, their dance of love around him again, but this time, curiously, they move in a different place or, as they call it, direction.

We watch them carefully and we see our brother, Shem, fade and now there is only a shimmering light. Now the maidens stop their dance and come into oneness, embracing the light.

We are so filled with questions in our many, multiple places within us and we look at one another with loving humor, but we remain very quiet.

We hear Lom-Sa slowly saying to us in a very beautiful tone (it sounds almost like the vibrations of the colors) and we know that we are to move again back to the Heaven Place and back to the Sacred Symbol.

We are delighted, as we feel the rushing energies moving all throughout us, and there we are! We look about with wonder, and listen to Yo-El and we hear his instructions that we shall be still and move to the points from whence we began.

The brethren of the Shining One surround us, curiously, and guide us from the Heaven Place up into the Father's Word.

Here, they move back a bit so that we can be as we would, and we begin to communicate questions about what were these things and why was that in the manner that it was, and on and on we question and explore and use our knowing-things and all that.

We gather together with Yo-El, Lom-Sa, Nov'A, and we look for the others, but they seem to have moved off a bit. So we come into a closeness to Shem-El and the others.

He sayeth to us, "You have questions and I have only some answers, but here are the answers that I have," and he calls us to become one that he can give to us his knowing.

"Are we to be like them if we have this knowing?" one of our brethren asks, and it seems as though that question summons our brother, E-Ude, back to our grouping. We are joyful for this.

It is E-Ude who states to us very softly and with the Father's love and light, "It cannot be so. It is only that which is in accordance to their choices and that which they have builded, but it cannot make you do or be that which you do not wish to be."

One of our brothers comes forward and asks of E-Ude, "I believe you, my dear brother, but how is it that some of the other of our brothers appears to be ..." and we wait as our brother struggles to express this. "He appears to be one with the No-Place Earth. He seems to be one of them now. He doesn't seem to know us anymore."

We feel that thing wanting to come and be and express itself, and we tell it we do not wish it to be so and the thing goes away. We laugh a bit, and we listen as E-Ude speaks to us.

"What I have learned from the brethren who have been with E-Am and Nov'A is that they have built (evolved, they call it) a structure that is at the level that we know to be the knowing-thing, the thinking-thing. And they call this the mind."

We look upon one another with wonder. What a nice word they have chosen in their word-things.

"How does this mind-thing make him not know us or want to be with us anymore?"

We feel our brother's love questioning.

E-Ude continues, "This is a part of what they have chosen, and they have chosen it with some force, some power."

We ask E-Ude to become one with us that we can have the knowing of what he is giving to us, and we do. As we move into our uniqueness, afterwards, we are dizzy with the breadth and depth of the confinement of expression and how it has ... and we realize that we do not wish to know it anymore for now. We choose from the time and movement-thing of the Earth, with humor, and we come into oneness, that we can simply be in the joy and wonder of our Father. We move towards the colors with such gayety and love for one another that all things that were, are now in harmony within us.

We come to the colors and, again, it seems as though they know that we are coming to them for their gifts and they are reaching out to us, and we look upon them with such love, for their sweetness is as the Father's touch. We move into the first rivulets of the beautiful color and they spin all throughout our beings. We find much to laugh about and we begin to sing songs as the colors continue to spin about within us and about us. Then, other colors come and soon the colors of the Father's words, as these are expressing in the multiplicity, are dazzling us.

We go to our Sacred Place within and we open ourselves, that all of the gifts the Father has given us can receive of the Father's Word and colors and the multiplicity of their expression. We realize now that there is no limit, none of the barriers or definements ... how do they call it ... definitions of limitation, of form. Here, the Father's Word keeps expanding and we feel the multiplicity of the Father's Word resounding within us and without.

Now we must sing songs and dance dances in honor of this, and so we do. We come into oneness and then we move out into our uniqueness as we soar about in the colors, moving in a grouping, then in oneness, then singularly as the others watch with wonder and joy the beauty of our Father's gifts to us.

Then we come to a place where we feel the colors enveloping us like the Father has placed His arms about us, but it is the colors of His Word that do this. We feel as though the Father is, Himself, embracing us. So we go inward to the Sacred Place, in oneness, together, and we take these blessings of the Father into our being.

Some say, "Let us gather up these blessings and place them within the Sacred Place, that, should ever there be that experience where such a blessing is a good thing to give, we can do so."

So, it seems that the greater do we gather up portions of the Father's embrace, the greater does it come. We find such delight in this that we cannot resist ...

We go into our oneness and awaken the Sacred Place within and sayeth, "Father, this is such a wonderful thing that You have given us!"

And we wait.

Then the Father can be heard,

It is an expression of my love for you, my sweet Children. Take of it as you would. It is now such that it will never end. And the greater you take of it and give of it, the greater shall it be.

We are in wonder over this!

One sayeth to the Father, "This is such a wonderful gift. May we take it with us within?"

The Father smiles upon him and reaches out to embrace him, and we all feel the embrace along with him.

Then, the Father looks upon him as they become unique. We find humor in this, for we know that, in this, the Father is always within us, so this expression of Him moving into uniqueness is such a beautiful thing to behold! We love it, because we can go to Him as we would a brother or a sister *and embrace Him!*

So we do. We all rush to the Father and we embrace Him mightily, and in our oneness we all feel His embrace in return. To our delight, we feel the Father moving us within His embrace. We look about as He moves us and we see the wonder of expressions of His Word, and we find such rapture in this. Then the Father comes to a pause and releases us from His embrace, and we are so joyful.

One sayeth to Him, "Oh, Father, that was so beautiful. Thank You."

The Father sayeth,
You are welcome, my children.

He asks again, "Father, might we do this again?"

The Father sayeth to him very gently,
You are my sweet son whom I love dearly. You and your brethren may come here to this part of my Word as it unfolds.

And, if you become one in the manner as you have and in the joy call me from your Sacred Places, in oneness, I shall be with you and we shall do this beautiful dance again.

We are so joyful for this and we ask the Father, "Sweet Father, may it be so that we can, in one of their times, bring that of these gifts that we have gathered and placed within the Sacred Place within us … May we take these to them and give them as You have gifted us?"

The Father gives us a light of knowing and we feel it and know from what He has given that it will come to pass that we can give to them, as they are willing to receive it. We ponder this, but we do not wish to give it our light, our being, and so we place it within for another journey.

The Father sayeth to us more and then we hear Him say,
Be about those experiences, now, that call to you and that you feel vibrate as you have known this within you, and do as you wish, as you choose … and, be joyful.
Remember, I am ever with you.

We hear E-Am and Nov'A and Yo-El and many of the others, and we move to our uniqueness to listen to them.

One of our brethren goeth to them and sayeth to them,

"We have gathered beautiful gifts and we have had such wondrous times with our Father. May we go into oneness with you all and give you these?"

Nov'A's light becomes so beautiful, and we hear her say, "Yes, of course," and glances at the others, and beckons unto us.

So we move into oneness and give this to these, our brethren, and they are experiencing it as we have experienced it.

Then, we move to our uniqueness, and we feel the call in the knowing of Yo-El and E-Am and Nov'A and E-Ude. From our oneness with them we have the knowing of their intention, and we say to them, "We will give to you what we have to give."

"None among us wishes to go into the No-Place Earth as you have done, Yo-El. We wish to keep our love for our brethren there, all of them, everyone of them," and we see the knowing of our brother who speaks, and he sayeth to them, "When there is that time, as the Father has told us (that we have given to you) then we will journey there. But we do not see this from our knowing with you to be, as they call it, that time."

Yo-El moves very close to this one. We see their love for one another envelop them both, and we find such a joy in this.

Then they move to their uniqueness and we hear Yo-El say, "It is, of course, always that we honor your choice, as the Father has sayeth to us to honor the choice of those in the Earth. We have made our choice: that we shall seek to free our brother, Shem (who is called by the Father, Shem-El) and return him to his uniqueness here. We wish to set him free."

There cometh the call from the Shining One and so we all gather into oneness. But our oneness has a different feeling, and we are puzzled by this. So, we give our love to one another as we move into the All.

We are embraced by the Shining One and AoLe'A, and many, many of our brethren who are with the Shining One.

After some experiences, we gather together to communicate with each other in our uniqueness.

Some in our grouping come forward and say, "We have learned a great deal from our journeys, and from the knowing that you have given us, Yo-El, AoLe'A, and You, dear Brother." (We look at him express this to the Shining One.) "But we say to You … What is it that is this unique thing that we feel, even now in our oneness?"

The Shining One sayeth to us, *"It is a part of the knowing, and the knowing is, in a sense, calling to you, for in the knowing are discoveries. While you would not see these in the present as gifts, they are very much as gifts, where they will build within you a Knowing that is called, again, Understanding. With Understanding, and Knowing, and the experiences comes a beautiful brilliance of a gift: And all of this together as I have just given it to you is called Wisdom."*

Many of us look to one another back and forth.

Finally, Dan-El steps forward and sayeth to the Shining One, "What need do we have of this, this wisdom-gift? I am very joyful and I feel love from all of you and from the Father. I find such joy in the colors and we had a beautiful journey with the Father. Why should I have this wisdom thing?"

Oh, we feel the beauty of Dan-El and we see it reflecting back and forth from the Shining One to he.

The Shining One sayeth very sweetly, *"You have the right of the Father's gift of choice. It is only that I tell you of this that you might know it, and if you wish that it would grow and become wisdom, then that is your choice. But you are correct… You do not need it. There is no such here as a need; it is that which they have fashioned in the Earth No-Place."*

Dan-El reflects upon this. We can see him take it to his Sacred Place and then he brings it forth again. "I see that it has its own unique gifts to give to us, but I also see in the Sacred Place that the Father's light showeth to me that these are things that are needed when one journeys in the definitions of the No-Place. What need have I of wisdom here, where I am one with my brethren and with my Father's Word?"

Then there is one of those beautiful silence-things as we all feel this. We can feel the resonance of truth in it and it is most beautiful.

"It is as you say," the Shining One answers. "Choose as you would."

We feel a bit of something here, but we know that it is not of that righteous-thing to give to Dan-El now, for he seeks it not.

So, Dan-El embraces the Shining One and turns to move back into oneness with our grouping.

AoLe'A sayeth to us, "Be in your beauty, in your glory of God and His mighty gifts to you, of such light and such harmony within you, and if these are your choices, then so be it; and if you should have a call within to seek out as the sweet Shining One has said to you, then it shall be so."

We reflect upon this for a time and we see that some of our brethren ... our sweet, loved, cherished brethren ... are focusing upon another journey to the No-Place.

We speak with Dan-El and say to him, "We wish to support our brethren. If we can do the freeing-thing of our brother, Shem, who is Shem-El, then would it not be a good thing to do this?"

Dan-El agrees with us.

So we rejoin them, and now they begin to make choices on how they shall seek to free our brother, Shem.

12

A Brother Comes Home

"Gather with me, my brothers and sisters," sayeth the Shining One, *"and let us awaken, within the Sacred Place within us, a oneness."*

So, they gather together those who shall journey in the freeing of Shem, and the Shining One looks upon them all with a love and joy that bespeaks of the Father, Himself. After a time, the Shining One sayeth to us, *"My sweet brethren, within each of us is that oneness with the Father that is ever perfect and complete. Of this you know to some degree. Now I shall come to place within the Sacred Place that which the Father has given to me that I might gift you; that wheresoever thou art and whatsoever you are about, go to the Sacred Place and touch this Mark that I give you in His Name, and we shall be as we are now: one."*

We feel the presence of the Shining One within us, glowing within the Sacred Place, rightfully so, beside our Father. We know this in the *knowing* of it, and we take it all throughout that which is our uniqueness, that we might, each one, bear this, in honor and sweet joy, in service with this, our dear Brother.

It comes to completeness, and we move to our uniqueness and embrace one another. We go unto the grouping who has chosen, along with Dan-El, to support us in these works with their love and their light, and they give to us the lines-of-light, that we might ever know they are with us.

All of us, together, move to the Heaven Place.

The brethren of the Shining One rejoice as He comes unto them, each one, to celebrate again the oneness of service and the gifts of the Father that are ever present to be claimed.

Much is given and much is shared. We speak with E-Am, and AoLe'A, and Nov'A, and Cel'A, and all the others. We smile with them in the joy of loving them, and they smile upon us in return.

So we gather, now, as Yo-El calls to us that he is at the ready to make the journey.

The Shining One comes unto each of us again to bless us and they pause, together ... the Shining One and Yo-El, and all the others.

Then, we move to the Sacred Symbol and we claim the power of it in the opening of the pathway, as we move with ease through the varying elements, past the works that are now underway in between the elements. We ponder these as we see them, but we release this into the Knowing Place, that we might ponder it later.

With exhilaration, we pass through our Father's sacred River of Light and we take unto ourselves His continual love.

Now we approach the No-Place Earth and we feel that essence within us that wants to call us unto itself, and we look about and we see so many of our brethren feeling the same. In our oneness, now, we strengthen ourselves and we feel the complete peace of being in this oneness.

We look upon the additional *works*, as they call it, which have been completed upon the No-Place Earth and we see the energies of their creation living on in their works, and these are, indeed, works of great beauty. We can see how it is that they might find such a ... We know not what to call this, but something, which calls to them and they answer it, for it, is, indeed ... These works are beautiful.

As we approach the closeness to the No-Place Earth, we feel a tingling within our consciousness and we want to laugh with joy, but Lom-Sa looks at us with a smile and we do the quiet-thing very, very well.

Still, we feel it, and we touch one another, that we each know of the feeling and know our oneness, and we realize it is the closeness to our brethren whom we love so dearly. The essence of them wants to speak to us, we think, but we cannot be sure and we know that (from within the quiet-thing) this is not to be done.

We feel Yo-El and the others moving us towards where Shem has told them in their oneness. We look upon the No-Place Earth and we see the wonder of the curious works and the patterns and such as they have put in place here. Many of them, we see them moving into and out of, like they have created a large shell for themselves to move into and out of. We ponder this, and we agree that we shall call it from this place of Knowledge and do the thinking about it later.

Some of these shells are very beautiful and we see that they appear to be, each one, striving to make their shells more beautiful than the next. We smile upon this with wonder and ponder, why do they not all live in one shell? It is a glance from our dear brother that calls us back to the quiet-thing with deliberateness.

So we claim our oneness and we focus upon Yo-El. We see him preparing and we give to him all that we are, that he might use this in the preparation, for we know that he will engage the No-Place Earth. We touch the Sacred Place within us and we feel the Mark of our dear Brother and we feel as though He touches us. We smile unto the quiet-thing and we know that Yo-El knows this.

It is curious for us to observe, for Yo-El is here and yet, there he is, upon the Earth-Place, moving with us, passing by the others of our brethren who are in the … We do not understand it, but it is in the No-Place Earth, work-thing. He passes them by and only a few seem to pause for a moment, perhaps in feeling his presence for a moment. They do nothing but continue with their work-things.

We see now that, on the periphery of our brother Shem-El are Nov'A and Cel'A. Cel'A is moving about to be in a position opposing our sweet sister Nov'A, and the third sister is behind. Now we come, as we observe them, to realize that they are moving into more and more of the Earth-Place No-thingness. A rush of energy passes through us. We pause to do the quiet-thing, and we move to be one with Yo-El.

Yo-El glances to the left and right of his place in the No-Place Earth to perceive his sisters embracing him and knows the third is behind. So, before him is the opening that he has chosen to seek out our brother.

He cometh to a place where many of our brethren are gathered together in somewhat close proximity. We see him pause and, curiously, he makes himself known to those who are in the No-Place Earth.

Some look up with a start and others only glance over at him. Yo-El gathers up elements from the portions that are placed in the things and places them over the periphery of his being. When he does this, those who are of note to him relax and look back to their work-things.

So he moves, our brother, with fragments, little particles of the elements that have been woven into the work-things of the Earth, and he moves closer and closer until he is moving in and amongst the groupings. Most do not pay much heed to him, for it appears and feels as though he is quite similar to those of the brethren who are busied about their work things.

Lom-Sa looks upon us with a radiance of love and we know that he means to give to us an absolute peace, that what we are giving to our brother and sisters is of that pure peace. So, we do this from the quiet-place-thing.

Yo-El comes up to a small grouping of our brethren

and one of them, a rather tall fellow who is in the center of the grouping, brightens up so visibly that we can see him very clearly. Yo-El gestures with his hand-thing to calm this, and immediately our brother calms his light, for some of the others in other groupings have obviously noticed this. They are looking now, very carefully, at this grouping and our brother, Yo-El.

We claim very much quiet in the quiet-thing and giving peace with all of the peace that we have to give, and it seems to be effective. Those who had been started by the light have calmed and have turned back to their work things. It is curious to observe them. They seem to work in small groupings and shield their works from the other groupings, as though they are preparing something that is a very special gift that they wish to give to them without their knowing.

We smile upon this. But Lom-Sa gestures not to do any thing, so we do no thing from the quiet-thing. It is very easy for us to do this, for it requires naught. We look at one another and smile and we say to each other, *You are doing the quiet-thing very well,* and we do it even better.

Yo-El moves among the small grouping and we can feel the caution with which he doeth this. They glance at him with a curious sort of energy, as though they are not welcoming him, but, rather, putting some thing between themselves and he. He is not heeding this, but moving carefully within and out these barriers each of them are placing before themselves and he, and continuing to move very slowly and almost delicately to where our brother is.

It seems our brother is not as active in creating work-things as the rest, but he seems to be bearing elements or portions of the elements to them from which they are doing their work. So Yo-El moves up, close by our brother, and they glance at one another. We see the light and we know this one to be Shem.

Very slowly, our brother reaches his hand-thing up behind our sweet brother Shem and places it upon him. Instantly, we feel through our brother Yo-El a oneness with Shem. We feel the knowing he has gathered and we build a greater knowing and understanding. We see that this is moving into our Knowing Place, and we tell it to be very, very quiet: *Do the quiet thing there,* and it does.

We see them both bow their head things, as though they were communing in some way that we cannot discern.

One of the grouping who is off on the periphery has looked up and is studying the two of them very intently, so we intend to send some communiqué to our brother. But before we can Nov'A has moved into a position to be prepared to intercede if need be, but she does not. Obviously, Yo-El has said to her not to, and so she remains on the periphery, as do the other sisters.

Then, suddenly, there is the light of our brother Shem standing there.

All of the members of the grouping jump back with a start. We want to be there but we continue to stay in the quiet-place.

Shem-El is now showing his light, the light of the Father! Yo-El has moved to the side a bit, reverently.

The entities who are our brethren who know us not surround Shem-El, and they challenge him.

We can hear him say to them, "It is not that you can do unto I. I am of our Father, and now I depart from you to return to my Father."

To our wonder they throw things over our brother Shem-El, and for a moment we cannot see his light. Then, it comes to brilliance again.

Again, and again they attempt to place their things over Shem-El, and his light seems to separate them until they step back, gesturing and calling out with loud sounds and waving their tool-things from the work and such that they do. Others begin to come from other groupings to help them to quell this upstart, who is our brother Shem-El.

Before they can, the sisters do their dance-thing around the grouping and all of those who come to aid their brethren are bedazzled by it, it would seem. For they move slower and slower, and then they come to stand to look upon the wonder of our sisters as they create, with their movement, something that is of wonder in the No-Place Earth.

Then, it is Yo-El who reaches out to Shem-El and they become one and the light grows, and then the light is no more, as they claim the Sacred Symbol, and, suddenly, they are with us here.

The sisters simply leave that place, and the energy of their dance stays. All of those, our brethren who are in the sleep of the No-Place Earth work, try to reach out and touch it and grasp it, for it is of beauty. We know that they want to put this beauty of our sisters into their No-Place works.

The presence of our sisters, Yo-El, and Shem-El in the center of our grouping is almost more than we can ... well, hold ourselves to, in maintaining the quiet-thing.

Lom-Sa comes and gently sayeth to us, "Let us claim our oneness completely, all of us, and let us move to the Heaven Place, *now*."

Instantly we are in the Heaven Place, and we look upon one another with a great burst of laughter. Oh, Lom-Sa! How have you done this thing? It is wondrous." Lom-Sa only nods and smiles.

We all energize the points on the sacred symbol. Then the brethren of the Shining One come to embrace us all. The Shining One comes with AoLe'A, and they give homage of love and compassion and gratitude for Shem-El's great service unto these works.

We all move together into our Father's Word and we celebrate, first with the peace of our love for the Father as we all reach within the Sacred Place from our oneness, and we call the Father.

The joy of it bursts forth within and without each of us and we give it to one another in such a celebration.

The Father touches each one of us to acknowledge our joy and He gives of His love to us and we cherish this. We place His love in the Sacred Place within, and each of us begins to glow more and more. The beauty of our uniqueness shineth forth and dazzles one another with its brilliance. It is as a collage of the Father's colors at the edge of His Word that have come forth from within each of us to do the sacred dance of love. So we submit ourselves to oneness and we do the dance and sing songs. And Shem-El stands at the center, his being reaching out to touch all of us, and we know him to be a very sweet and loving brother.

All of the other of our groupings of brethren come from the distant places within our Father's Word and join with us, and celebrate the return of a brother from the No-Place Earth.

So it goes ... And so it goes ...

Then there cometh that experience wherein Il-Em comes forward to greet a brother who has, as he, journeyed into the No-Place Earth and returned ... as have we, indeed, but exceptionally so our brother, Yo-El, and our sisters who have literally, as they say it, walked upon its surface.

We move into our Sacred Places and our oneness that we can know of what they exchange with each other, and we become one with them.

Il-Em sayeth to our brother Shem, "You have journeyed long in that experience, my brother. Know that you have gained much, for I see the light of wisdom within you."

Shem-El nods, taking Il-Em into oneness with himself and giving of the wisdom to he, and then to Yo-El and all the others.

When all of this is complete, Shem-El looketh upon the Shining One who smiles and nods. Shem-El sayeth, "You already have this wisdom, do you not?"

The Shining One sayeth with such sweetness, as we can barely contain, "I have it, my sweet brother, given of the Father that I might serve in the manner as I do. But you, my dear brother, have gained this through the knowing of it. And through the knowing of it, it is now yours in a manner that is very unique to you. Therefore, I honor you, my brother,"

And Shem-El repeats, "And I honor You."

AoLe'A comes over to Shem-El and they become one, and then Nov'A and Cel'A and our third sister come to give their blessings to he and receive his in return.

"You have done a very, very good work, my sisters," sayeth Shem-El to them, "For you have given of the energies, as they call it, of your uniqueness. These are those energies that they use for birthing that which they conceive."

The sisters look upon one another with great affection, and to our wonder, they understand him.

We quickly look in our Knowing Places and in our Knowledge Places, but we cannot find this. So we move to oneness and prepare to ask them to give this to us, but we await, for they are continuing on.

The sisters are sharing with Shem-El and the Shining One and AoLe'A. We feel their sharing completely, and now we understand.

Yo-El brings Dan-El, E-Ude, and all of the others to the forefront and turns to reach for the Oneness with Il-Em, whom he has called forth from the No-Place and who is now ever with him, and he turns to E-Am and embraces him into oneness. And they stand there, the three of them, in this beautiful light. Then, they claim their uniqueness as they go before the Shining One, Shem-El, and the sisters. We hear them say, "What has been given here is not of we, but of our Father's love for all of His children. And we know that you have called us, sweet brother, Shem-El. Thus, we were honored to answer,"

Turning then to look upon the Shining One, Yo-El asks with gentleness, "What, my sweet Brother, of all of the others of our brethren? I saw them, I touched many of them through the elemental cloak that I wore, and I long for them, as do we all. Is there naught that we can do lest they call to us? Is it not so, my dear Brother, that they are merely covered with these same cloaks of elemental dust or fragments or something of this nature that has been fashioned so as to prevent them from remembering?"

The Shining One grows in His luminosity of love and He reaches up with His light and makes contact with Yo-El, who becomes radiant with the light of his Brother, and then, as such, to E-Am, and to Il-Em, and to E-Ude, to the sisters, to Shem-El, and to all of us. We feel this wondrous light, and it brings to us a special gift, which we know is from the Father.

So we dwell in this gift, this light, until Yo-El sayeth to Him, "What do you call this beautiful gift, my sweet Brother?"

The Shining One sayeth to him, *"It is the Father who has called this as that which is ever aright: it is the gift of Righteousness. Now it is yours, all of you. I say in answer to you, again, my brother ... There shall come a time when I and my brethren shall be within this gift of Righteousness to go unto the No-Place Earth and bring to it the light, that those who have lost their way and are covered in the illusion might know of it. That, I call my time, and it is not yet."*

There is a feeling that we all know and that we are familiar with, and we tell it to go back where it came from, for we want only joy, not the thing's energies.

The Shining One smiles on us brightly, for He knoweth what we have done and He gives to us His knowing of it that we have done well. *"If you wish to journey again to the No-Place Earth, you have that right, as do they, to choose. And now you know the Father's gift of Righteousness. Within it is His truth, His honor, His love and compassion. This maketh up that which is the power that can create and make all things in their perfection, as the Father has given it.*

"Take this gift then, for you need naught else from I or my brethren. When my time has come, as they call it, I shall call you, my brethren. And you and we shall journey together and bring the light of Righteousness into the No-Place Earth, that those who are lost can choose.

"Now, I shall depart with AoLe'A and my brethren into the presence of my Father's Cloak. But you may do now as you are guided. Remember to touch the Mark I have given you, and we are immediately one. May our Father's peace be that which ever nourishes you and gives you the rebirthing of life in the form of His Word wheresoever you might be, and whatsoever you may be about. Fare well for now, my sweet brother and my sweet brethren."

We look upon them with wonder and awe, for their light comes into oneness and grows larger and larger. Then, with a gentle sound and a soft movement of energies, they are gone.

Oh-h ... We look upon one another and we feel that thing come, striving to do a dance around us. We look to the light of each other and the sweet gift of the Father called Righteousness. We pull this to the forefront and it gives to us the strength of our uniqueness and our oneness.

We turn to look at the thing as it dances crazily about us, and we speak unto it, "Be thou gone from this place.

Knowest thou not this to be holy? Return when you are ready to receive our light. Until then, come ye not again."

That thing breaks up into many tiny pieces that go dizzily wobbling off towards the No-Place Earth, and we know that we shall see it no more.

We encircle our brothers and sisters with our love and our completeness as we see them moving within, to their Sacred Places, in a state of oneness. We know that they are doing that contemplation-thing in the holy-of-holies within their own beings, and we surround them and claim the gift of Righteousness, that our light nourishes them as the Shining One has nourished us.

We know that we are moving now, gently moving off into our Father's Word. We can feel the presence of others of our brethren in groupings here and there who give to us gifts of love, and we return these with a touch of the gift of Righteousness, and we see them dance with joy.

We move in such a sweet peace, and we come nigh unto the edge of the colors, and we pause. We move into the peace of oneness, surrounded by the gift of our Father's Righteousness, and here we dwell for a long experience.

The Guardian's call is soft at first, but it passes all throughout our being in our oneness, and we see our sweet brethren in the center of our oneness stir a bit. The Guardian's call becomes stronger and stronger.

Finally, our brethren, led by our brother Yo-El and all the others, move into their uniqueness. Their radiance is magnificent as we look upon them, and we know they have taken the gift of Righteousness and made it their own uniqueness. We look to one another and very quickly we do the same, and in this way, our oneness is yet complete.

Yo-El sayeth, "Let us answer our sweet Guardian's call."

So, in our oneness, we move, and Lom-Sa sayeth, "We are with the Guardian, *now*."

We delight with great joy that we are, as he sayeth the word, there before the Guardian. We go to him and we touch him with joyful love and humor. He smiles upon us, and we say to him, "What is it that you doeth?"

He looks with a gentle knowing and sayeth to us, "Sweet brethren, what you hear is from within you, as well. You have only but to call it forth and then it is yours, and as you call it forth and know it, then use it, as have I. That is all. What I have, as you see me, you have. Each of us in our uniqueness brings special qualities of that together in our oneness. Look you within and see the power of our Father's Word."

So we look at one another in wonder. Some of us look within the others, and we see the Father's Word. We tell them where it is, and they call forth the Father's Word, and we have great laughter. And we all call forth the Father's Word, and we embrace it.

Then, we listen as we hear the Guardian speak. "You have learned much, my sweet brethren, have you not?"

Yo-El answers him very quickly, "We have, indeed. But I suspect (with clarity, I might add) not nearly what you know and what you have within,"

The Guardian sayeth with a quick bit of lightness, "All that I have is yours if you ask for it. But what am I that thou are not?" They look at one another, and Yo-El finally states, "I see that you have the power of choice … that you have chosen this unto the Father, that you shall evermore be the Guardian here. So, I honor this and I give to you that which I have to give that it might be yours in any way that you should choose to use it in service to our Father and to our brethren."

The Guardian looks upon Yo-El and touches him and acknowledges the intent and the sweetness of the gift and we hear him say, "I accept your gift with honor to you. And I say to you, there shall come to pass those experiences wherein I shall give to you that which you have given to me, that your journey shall be made with greater ease and that you shall endure in the face of that which would seek to cloak you."

Yo-El pauses for a moment as we can feel this and, then, very quickly, he looks with love and honor to the Guardian and sayeth, "I accept that which you shall give to me, and we are one." He moves into the Guardian's embrace and they become one.

We laugh and dance with great joy, for when they become one, we become one, and we all, together, feel the glory of these beautiful expressions of our Father's Word ... in the form of the Guardian, in the form of Yo-El, and in each of our forms. So do we celebrate our own being, along with the being of all of our brethren.

We experience this for a long experience, for it is good.

Then, the Guardian sayeth to Yo-El and to those who are close to him, "Go forth, then, and contemplate as you have, and do as you feel guided. And choose that which is as the Father's gift to you to be that which guides you. My blessings go with you all."

Suddenly, we see the Guardian no more. But we know he is ever present. So we move in our oneness once again to the edge of the colors.

Yo-El and Nov'A, E-Am, and Cel'A and all of the others say to us, "Let us claim our uniqueness, dance and sing among the colors, celebrate our love for our Father and bathe ourselves in His gifts. Let us do this now."

And so we do.

13

Reaching EuDe'E

There is a considerable contemplation as we review what our Guardian has given to us and spoken to this, our brother. We contemplate these things from the Knowing and Thinking Places, and we call them forth that we might look upon them and that of the experiences we have known.

Yo-El sayeth to us, "What thinkest thou of these events, dear Lom-Sa? Explain to us what you know, for I see the knowing in you about the Sacred Symbol and your calling forth the movement in the manner as you have."

We move into joyful oneness and encircle our sweet brother, Lom-Sa. We look upon his light and his knowing, and feel the goodness of it and the love that he carries with him for our Father.

"There is much within our sweet Father's Word, as I have come to know it in the experiences as we have journeyed and in my contemplations. I see within the Sacred Symbol much more, and I feel and hear in our Father's Word each time we journey into the beautiful colors that there is that which can be known if we would still ourselves to feel it and know it at that Place which is Sacred within."

Dan-El comes forward unto him and asks, "Can you show us? Can you take us to this? Or can we become one with you and know it?"

Lom-Sa smiles upon him and embraces him with his love and the light of the two of them become one. We laugh upon this with love.

Then, Dan-El sayeth as he claims his uniqueness, "I see what you mean," and he steps back into our grouping and we see as he has seen.

Yo-El sayeth unto him, "Lom-Sa, would it be well for us to know this to a greater level? For as we have journeyed in the Sacred Symbol, I have felt these ... shall I call them *gifts of light* in our Father's Word, that appear as we journey within the Sacred Symbol."

"Yes," Lom-Sa states softly with his love shining upon Yo-El. "I think this to be good."

So we gather into oneness, and off we soar across the Father's Word, laughing, singing songs, until we come unto the colors.

Lom-Sa sayeth to us, "Let us make the Sacred Symbol here on the periphery of the colors as they are dancing and singing their song to us."

So we do, and the Light cometh again, that Light which is of the Father, yet sayeth nothing and doeth nothing but gives to us a pathway in which we can choose.

Some of the choices we now see in their magnificence. So we move into the Sacred Symbol and Lom-Sa guides us. We feel these. We look upon them and we experience them, and we see how they blend with one another and how we can move along pathways that we have not known.

We come into a color, and we laugh and sing unto the color. It sings to us in return. We feel the color's gifts and we laugh all the more, and our laughter seems to bring joy to the color. The color shifts and undulates and passes through us, all through us, and rings out in the Sacred Place within us in such a delightful way. We thank the color.

We move now on a different pathway and we feel the singing on the pathway. We look ahead and see the beautiful lights of a movement of kaleidoscope, as they call it, where the colors are actually communing with one another and singing with one another. We move into them and they embrace us. They awaken something within us, and we feel it. Here is a feeling, and another, and another, and so forth. We look upon these and we find them very,

very beautiful, and we ponder them, for they are as parts of our own being.

And E-Ude sayeth to Nov'A, "You look very beautiful in these colors." And Cel'A comes forward and we see her beauty, and then we see that of E-Am, and all the others in a different, wondrous way. The colors of the Father's Word seem to have expressed themselves in yet another form and they are as liquid moving through and particles and song, and we continue experiencing these different pathways with great joy and delight.

After many experiences, we come together in our Sacred Places, and we call out to the Father, "Father, we wish to give to You the joy that we have gathered from these experiences."

The Father comes with a great burst of joyful laughter and He touches us all and we embrace Him.

As He strokes the beauty of one and then the next, and the next, and each of us, we say to Him, "Father, we have found the many magical pathways in the Sacred Symbol. We have not known these previously. Could You tell us why this is?"

The Father looks upon that one who is speaking and reaches out to embrace him, and they become one. Then our brother comes forth from the Father, filled with the radiance of the Father's love and blessings.

The Father sayeth to us all,

There is much for you, my sweet Children ... many places, many colors, and many pathways, and these are all my love for you, awaiting your discovery should you choose to find them.

You are complete in this very moment, so do not think that these things are something that you need to find; they are merely that that is intended to bring you joy and the knowing of my love for you.

Yo-El comes forward to the Father and sayeth, "Father,

the Sacred Symbol is so magnificent and yet, as the Shining One has shown it to us, I feel within the Sacred Place within me that these pathways are likened unto the Sacred Symbol, that they would afford us the greater understanding and movement and discovery. What more, I do not know, Father. I only hear the call of them."

The Father places His hand upon our brother with great love, and sayeth,

The call that you hear is your own uniqueness, my sweet son. It is unto you that I give my love and blessing, that you might ever feel the right of your freedom to follow those calls as they bring you purpose and joy to so do.

"Oh, Father, thank You so much for this, and I know You give this to us all as always. But I feel something, Father."

The Father looks upon him with a gentleness.

Speak, my son.

So he does. "Father, when we answered our brother Shem's call and I felt the energies that were being used to try to quell my presence and Shem-El's ... within those energies I saw my brethren and they are so beautiful, my Father. I know that You know within me what I wish, and I ask You now, is this of Righteousness, as it has been given to us, that I might do this thing?"

Then, the Father brightens even more and His light shineth upon Yo-El, and we gather very close to the Father and Yo-El that we might feel His light and understand.

Remember what you have been given and what I have spoken to you and your Brother, whom you call the Shining One, and the others: As long as you honor your brothers and sisters, you may follow that which calls to you. But this you know. I see the knowing in you, and I ask you now, my sweet son, why is it that you ask this of me?

Yo-El pauses for a moment and does that Contemplation-Thing, and we look upon him with wonder, for we see something we hadn't noted before. Then, swiftly, he brings it forth to give unto the Father.

The Father pauses as He embraces all of us even closer. Then He sayeth,

All of you, my sweet Children, have something within you, as Yo-El has brought forth. It is that light of beauty and uniqueness that is yours alone and that makes you as beautifully unique as you are.

Within that uniqueness is something very special for each of you. It is the nature of your uniqueness. And it will ever guide you if you seek it and listen. It is in the Sacred Place within you, where I dwell, as well. This is what I cherish of you and I ask of you to cherish it, as do I.

Yo-El, follow that which calls to you in the light of Righteousness, and as thou knoweth, even as you have spoken it to me, My love and My light are with you. This is so for all of you, my Children.

Here, take this. It is of My Word, and if you place it within you, it will always be that which can be called forth to bring you comfort.

So, I leave you now, my Children, for yours is the joy of experience and knowing. Be about those things and those gifts that await you. Know My love to be yours forever.

The Father moves away from us, and there is such a beautiful collage of sound and light and color and many more things that we have not given name to, and we delight in them.

On the No-Place Earth some of the brethren who had been in the groupings and who had been passed by as

Yo-El journeyed there have gathered together in one of their shells, and they have come into a very close order.

One of them sayeth to the others, "Did you see it?"

And one of them answers, "I not only saw it, I touched him."

"What was it like?" the others ask.

"It was beautiful. He became illuminated with something that resonated within me."

Another in the grouping cautions him to be very careful, for some of the others might know of that which he is giving forth.

"I feel something," one of them sayeth. "I feel something that I saw in our brother Shem, and then he was gone."

They all agree that something calls to them, and they come close together that they can dwell in the vague memory of their sweetness that seems in a very subtle way, to beckon unto them.

Some distance away, others who are of the No-Place Earth are also in discussion, and they speak about this with anger and how they can prevent this from occurring again, for they are sure that it will disrupt things.

As we look upon these events and many more, we move back to our brethren who are in the Word of our Father, and we see the knowing of it growing within Yo-El.

He speaks of it. "Brethren, have we not made a pathway unto the No-Place Earth using the Sacred Symbol?"

We all look upon one another and we call back the experience and look upon it carefully. Then we answer him, "Yes, it does appear that a pathway has been made,"

Dan-El asks Yo-El, "Is it yet intact?"

Yo-El turns to Lom-Sa, who answers with a nod, "That which you have created remains until you choose it not."

Yo-El brightens up and states, "Is it always so?"

Lom-Sa smiles broadly, "You know this. Until one chooses to set it free, it is as you have called it to be."

Another in our grouping comes forward and states, "Could they not use this pathway to come unto us, to seek to put those particles over us?"

Lom-Sa begins to laugh gently and goes to this one to embrace him. "Feel that?"

That one smiles greatly, "Yes, Lom-Sa, I feel it and I understand. If they come here on our pathway, we will embrace them with our love."

We all laugh and begin to sing songs and dance dances, and we move into some of the pathways and give these joyful experiences to some of the other colors and some of the other ... We have no name for them yet, so we will call them the No-Name Joys. Then we come back together, and we move about, swirling through the joy of our Father's Word.

Then, we come to a place where we decide to become one in the Contemplation-Thing. We look upon all these things with wonder, and we decide to dwell in them for a time. We move into the great peace of our Father's gifts and we become one with the Father and His gifts, and we call forth the Sacred Places within us and make them one in our oneness. But we do not call the Father.

Then, we feel it, and we look upon one another with wonder and we listen ...

We hear some calling.

Yo-El brightens up strongly and Lom-Sa touches him.

We move back into our Sacred Place of Oneness, and we hear ... Some of our brethren are calling us! Can it be? We look to one another with such awe and hopefulness. We seek Il-Em from our oneness, and we bring him to the center of our consciousness of oneness so that he can see the calls and know if they are true.

Il-Em looks upon them and he makes them unto himself. And then, with a smile of beautiful light he sayeth, "It is true."

So we move into our uniqueness, and we move with such joyful light to the Heaven Place, and there brethren of the Shining One come unto us with great wonder and joy, for they have known the call as well.

Yo-El goes before one of the Shining One's brethren and sayeth to him, "Knowest thou the number of Callers?"

He answers, "I cannot be certain, for some calls are very weak, as though they are few in number. Others are stronger; somehow they have begun to remember and they are calling, choosing, you see, to leave the No-Place Earth,"

Yo-El's light grows very bright, and Lom-Sa and E-Ude and Il-Em form a pattern around him and become one with him.

We see them in the Contemplation-Thing, calling forth the Sacred Light, and we move to become one and encircle them that we might know them and they us.

Then, as the experience passes, we move into oneness, our unique energies awakened, that we can share from the uniqueness of each and thereby gain much.

"I believe it to be in accordance with the Righteousness given to us to answer these calls. So, it is my intent to do so," sayeth Yo-El. "I know that they are already contemplating what has occurred with our brother Shem, and perhaps they are, in some way, seeking to prepare a better repulsion of us or resistance, as they might call it. I know not what this is, but I can feel it. See? Here it is."

He gives it unto us and we look upon it and see that it hasn't any life, in terms of freedom. It is very, very

Not-Living, and some of us wish to give our love to the Not-Living consciousness.

Yo-El states, "It is only that which is being discerned. Therefore, we must not do this thing. We have no right."

Much communing and sharing and joyful experiences are shared.

We move off into our Father's Word, that we can be in the purity of His love and grace, and we look upon all of this. In our uniqueness, we share greatly and we think upon it, that it is a righteous thing to answer these calls. And our love and longing for these our brethren, brothers and sisters in the No-Place Earth, grows very bright and comes to the forefront.

"We must keep ourselves in the completeness of our uniqueness," sayeth Yo-El, "lest we violate their right, as they have constructed it. As I have journeyed there already, perhaps I might be better to journey there, and you sustain the Sacred Symbol and the other paths that we have now with us. What thinkest thou of this, my sweet brother, Lom-Sa?"

Lom-Sa's light billows gently and embraces Yo-El and they become one, and Il-Em moves to become one with them, as does E-Ude and Nov'A and Cel'A and the third sister. We look upon one another and claim our oneness that we can become a part of them. And the experience grows to great beauty.

So, we begin to move again back to the Heaven Place, and we join with our brethren who are of the Shining One. We form the Sacred Symbol, this time with many more entities of our brethren, and beautiful brethren from other groupings who have heard this call. The Sacred Symbol is magnificent, and the uniqueness of our individuality is blended into a oneness. So, we move from the points to the center.

Lom-Sa sayeth, "Let us move, now, to the outskirts of the No-Place Earth."

Immediately we are there.

We strengthen our oneness within the Sacred Symbol that we can be complete and that nothing is incomplete in our being, and we look upon the paths. We choose one and move upon it, and as we do, we follow the light of the calls.

We see a grouping, and we pause and make our oneness positioned above this grouping. Not within the energies, but the No-Place Earth, itself.

The sisters move to the center of our oneness within the Sacred Symbol and they begin to move slowly in their song and dance. Yo-El and Il-Em move to the center of their dance. And all of them are gone.

Yet, they are here. We marvel at this, for they are both here and there, as before.

We see Yo-El moving slowly to touch the surface of the No-Place Earth, and Il-Em beside him.

The sisters are on the periphery at a distance. They are in their sacred dance, so we know that, unless they choose, the brethren of the No-Place Earth shall not know them.

Il-Em gathers up particles of the elements that they have been using for their work things and places them over Yo-El, and Yo-El doeth this over Il-Em. They look upon one another with a smile, but they make no laughter.

So they begin to move.

We can see the light of the Callers so very faint, and we feel that Thing that is surrounding them that we have sent back to the Earth-Place, or perhaps it is one of its kinfolk. With this, we laugh, but very carefully in our completeness.

We feel the touch of Lom-Sa with a smile again, pointing to the quiet-thing, so we do this with great vigor.

We marvel at how much on the outer-seeing of our brethren, Yo-El and Il-Em ... If we weren't *knowing* them, we might think they were brethren of the No-Place Earth. But now and then a bit of light can be seen. We see them moving to the shell, a sizeable one that we know the light of the call is in, and they seek entrance. We see the call almost gone, as our brethren within who are issuing the call are being very, very careful. Then, to our joy we see Yo-El and Il-Em have moved into the shell. It is very quiet. There is very little light coming. Then, slowly, we see the light growing, and we move into our oneness of knowing and we listen to them.

"You are he who came to our brother, Shem, are you not?"

"You know me?" answers Yo-El softly.

"I can feel something from you that I felt when you were here previously. What is it that you are? What is it that you do? We feel something,"

Yo-El looks at Il-Em, and Il-Em nods and moves very close to the grouping who seem to be very cautious with us.

Il-Em states, "I am one of you and this is my brother," gesturing to Yo-El. "I was as you are, but I remembered very clearly, and I called out, and this, my brother, Yo-El, heard my call and answered and lifted me up,"

"What do you mean, lifted you up?" one asks.

"Just as you saw your brother, Shem. I became as I am: of the Light. Then, I accepted my brother's hand, as you know the hand-thing, and he lifted me up. But in truth, it is I who chose to be as I am."

"And what is that?" asks one with a bit of challenge.

Il-Em looks carefully at Yo-El and they contemplate this, and Yo-El states, "Proceed Il-Em."

Il-Em reaches to the outer periphery of the particles of

elements and grasps them, as though they were some sort of covering likened unto those worn by the brethren in the No-Place Earth, and he slowly parts this.

Those of our brethren of the No-Place gasp and call out and make sounds, and Il-Em closes the outer covering again. Some are doing a weeping-thing. Others are trembling with great fear, that fear-thing that we saw before.

We feel what they are feeling, and we want to give to them of our love. But Lom-Sa reminds us, "Be very complete in the quiet-thing." So we work very carefully to keep the quiet-thing powerful.

Nov'A begins to sparkle and her light becomes evident, and then Cel'A the same, and then the third sister.

We ponder why they do this. They have positioned themselves around the shell in which our brothers are. Then, we see the reason ... A great number of the brethren of the No-Place are rushing towards the shell and, to our surprise, with the force of their movement, they surge past the sisters and cover the shell in which our brethren are preparing, again and again, with some elements that we have not seen.

The sisters are spinning about, but it seems to have little effect, and the covering grows and grows and we can no longer see the light of our brethren.

Lom-Sa states to us very softly and lovingly, "Do not let that thing come into our completeness. Look you here, into the center of our being. Here is that Light of our Father."

We look upon it and take it unto ourselves, and we feel the strength of our being and the Light of our Father's gift of Righteousness. We take His gift of the peace-thing and we place it over our love and our gifts that we wish to give, and Lom-Sa looks upon all of us with a joyful sweetness and smiles.

We see that much of the commotion that was taking

place has settled. Our sisters have moved off a distance from the mighty number of brethren who have come, literally ... Well, we don't know their terms, but they are of a goodly force, as they call it.

So, Lom-Sa comes to us again in his oneness with us and sayeth, "Now is the time for us to move to the Sacred Place within."

So we do, and we bring the power of the Sacred Place to the center of our oneness. The beauty of it begins to radiate, and we feel it and it gives to us a joy, and the joy that we feel, we send along the lines-of-light connecting us to our brothers and sisters on the No-Place Earth.

It is the sisters who first begin to grow, as they feel the light we are giving them, the sacred power of our Father's love. They begin to glow brightly, and we feel the light begin to come through the masses that have surrounded and placed their elements over the shell.

We hear them beginning to make their call-out-things, and they sayeth many of their words. They fearfully, as they call it, combat our light and yet it serves them to no avail. We feel what they call anger, and something else that is very much not-alive: not-free. We look upon this with curiosity, and we think about it and place it in the Knowing Place where we might later contemplate it. It is indeed, curious.

Then, the sisters begin their dance and they move closer and closer to the shell-thing. As they do, the brethren of the No-Place who have been seeking to make our brothers their own begin to move back, calling out loudly and waving their tool-things at our sisters. But our sisters focus upon one another, and the three of them form a beautiful orb of light.

Then, the light of our brothers, Yo-El and Il-Em, grows brightly.

We hear them again.

"Now it is your choice," Yo-El sayeth softly.

Some in the grouping have come to Yo-El and Il-Em, who have now shed the outer covering of particles of the elements, and embrace them mightily. Instantly, their light is as beautiful as our own! And, oh ... We want to sing with them and dance with them!

Lom-Sa whispers to us, "Remember the quiet-thing."

So, we do it pretty well, indeed.

Il-Em is embracing one of them with such sweetness, and we know from the line-of-light between us that Il-Em had to leave him behind when he took our brother Yo-El's hand-thing.

Then another, a sweet sister, comes and embraces Il-Em and our brother, and the light grows ... and another, and another. Now, all but one is claiming their light of the Father's gift.

We see Yo-El gently containing his light and moving over to be beside the one. "What is it, my sweet sister?"

"Oh," she begins, "I have so many sweet sisters and brothers. How can I leave them behind?"

Yo-El extends his hand to her and she places her hand-thing in his. "Feel this," he begins very softly. "I only offer to you. I do not do anything but offer. It is the way of our Brother, the Shining One,"

She looks up at Yo-El, and she feels something! "Tell me of Him."

"He is the One whose light is of the beauty of the Father, Himself. He is the One who has chosen to keep His oneness with the Father throughout all. We are the same as He, except that, as you, I, too, have had many experiences and many journeys. He needs these not. He knoweth as the Father knoweth because He has chosen it, so we honor this choice. I know that you feel Him, for look you ... Here is His Mark within me. See? In this Sacred Place. Take your hand-thing and place it upon that Mark, and you will remember."

"Oh-h …" She begins to do the weeping-thing. "If I do that, what of my sweet sisters and brothers?"

"You must choose," Yo-El states, "as must they. And when they are in the choosing-thing and ask, if we can, we will answer their call. But if you touch my Brother's Mark, here, you will hear His promise that He will come and offer to all in a time ahead, as you call it."

Very, very slowly, trembling, she reaches her hand-thing and the light of it touches the Mark, and the light gently moves along her hand-thing to embrace her.

We can feel her beginning to feel the peace of our Father's gift.

"Oh-h …" she moans softly, but with joy, "this is my Brother!"

"Indeed," Yo-El states. "He is the brother to us all."

She begins to brighten and brighten, and even Yo-El, in all the experiences he has known with us and we, as well, look upon her brightness and her beauty, and we are in the light of it and it seems that her light grows and grows. Finally, it appears she is complete.

Yo-El, still holding her hand-thing, looks upon her and he states, "I am Yo-El, son of God. How are you known?"

She answers sweetly, "I am known as EuDe'E, daughter of God."

In the swiftness of a moment's passing, as they measure it in Earth, our brethren, embraced by the light of our love and in the presence of Yo-El and Il-Em and surrounded by the sisters, rush up into our oneness within the Sacred Symbol.

We hear the calls from the brethren, who are dwelling in the Darkness-Place, calling out to us, and Lom-Sa sayeth, "They cannot perceive us. They call out to that which is their own creation and they believe that we are something that is not of blessing to them and they continue to build this so that they will have a stronger force and hold over the others. But when it is right, others will call and perhaps we shall return. But now I say to you, let us go to the Heaven Place ... *now*."

We feel little strange reactions of energy as we swiftly move through the elements ... and something else that they have created between the elements and we marvel at this!

But instantly, so it would be measured, we are within the Heaven Place, and we hear the singing and rejoicing of the Shining One's brethren. We move to the sacred points of our Symbol and we bring the completeness of the power and energies into harmony here, and the joy is beyond our capacity to take into ourselves.

The brethren of the Shining One surround us all and lift us up, that we can move off into the Father's Word.

Here, the light becomes so brilliant! The colors come and dance among us and bless all these of our brethren, our sisters and brothers, who have chosen to come from the No-Place Earth.

We move into oneness, and we feel the love of these brothers and sisters once again, and we sing mighty songs.

Others of our brothers and sisters come from all across the Father's Word to be one with us, and our light grows.

We have many, many experiences of love and peace and joy. And we laugh with each other, and we become one with each other again, renewing our completeness and feeling the wonder of it.

After a long experience, we come into oneness and we reach within and bring forth from our Sacred Place that which is our oneness from the Father's gifts.

Then, Yo-El comes to the center of our grouping, accompanied by Il-Em, Lom-Sa, the sisters, and many others. And they bring forth all of our brethren to stand before them and us, and the sisters form a circle around them with their dance and song.

And we call the Father.

First cometh the Shining One and AoLe'A.

Then cometh our Father, and we all rush to our Father, who surrounds us with His great Cloak of love and peace. He gives to us, and we give to Him.

Then we move to our uniqueness.

The Father looks upon us all and upon our brothers and sisters who have chosen to come out of the No-Place Earth. He smiles a smile of eternal love and touches each one, and turns to Yo-El and pauses to stand before him, not touching him. Then they become one, and we hear them laughing, so we become one with them and feel the laughter and the joy.

Then, the Father moves the middle of our grouping again and sayeth to us,

Peace and joy be with you, sweet Children. Be, unto yourselves, of great wonder and joy, for the beauty of your uniqueness and your choices have brought this great celebration unto being.

The Father moves from us, and we know that it is His intent that we share with one another the joys and wonders of this wondrous event.

Yo-El moves to be before the Shining One and AoLe'A, and then goes to bring EuDe'E to them. "I believe you know this Sister, for I see your light within Her." Smiling a smile of love and sweetness, he moves back a bit.

AoLe'A comes to EuDe'E and embraces Her mightily. Then, AoLe'A brings EuDe'E to the Shining One, and they begin to laugh softly and they do a dance together and sing a song together, and we all join them. Then cometh the others, one by one, to do the same with AoLe'A and the Shining One.

Many experiences are had, and our completeness grows because they have chosen to be free in the manner as our Father's Word goes forth. We cherish the beauty of them and we look upon the uniqueness of each one.

Then, after a long experience of joy and song and dance, the Shining One and AoLe'A sayeth to us, *"This is a very beautiful work you have done, in the manner as they call it in the Earth No-Place. But this is a work of your own individual beauty ... and not a work, but a sharing of that which is you. In the manner of this, call this as it is: the sharing of your Eternal Nature, which some call in some levels of the paths, the Eternal Nature of you. This Nature bears the gift of the Father, as you choose it. And look you ... in accordance with that which is the Father's Word, look you how your uniqueness has brought forth such beautiful goodness.*

"We return now to the Father's Cloak of Oneness, as we prepare with others of our brethren for that which is ahead. When that comes forth as a call, you shall know it, for I shall speak to you in your Sacred Place. Then, we shall come together and answer the Great Call.

"Be thou ever in the knowing of our love and our oneness. Remember my Mark, as I remember your beautiful uniqueness and love. Until then ..."

And they have gone ... not gone as in the No-Place Earth, we remind each other, but merely, they have followed one of the pathways and moved into the beauty of our Father's Cloak.

The sisters are rejoicing with the sisters from the No-Place Earth. It seems that EuDe'E is to them, the sisters of the No-Place, as Nov'A has become to our sisters ... meaning only that our sisters have been here in the experiences with us in their completeness.

So now we move in oneness off towards the colors, that we might gift them, as the Father has gifted us, with the beauty and wonder of who and what they are, that we may see their light and hear their song in the fullness of its potential.

Then sayeth Yo-El to us, "After a time, it is in my knowing that I shall bring my sister, EuDe'E, to the Guardian."

14

Into the Mind-Thing

We soar with joy about the Father's Word, feeling the wonder of it, feeling the love that flows constantly from within His Word. So do we take this unto ourselves and give it unto our brethren that we become one in our Father's love, and so do we soar.

We look now upon Yo-El and all the others gathered with them; then, we look upon the No-Place Earth and we see the many activities and events as are unfolding.

Now we journey into the sacredness of where the Shining One, our Brother, and all these who are with Him are dwelling in the glory and joy of being one with the Father in the Father's spirit form. As we look upon our Brother, we see the love that He has surrounded Himself with, as are AoLe'A and all the others, and we know the goodness of this and we see the preparation on the part of the others.

Then, as we hear our brother Yo-El speak, we return in that moment to him and the grouping gathered.

"I feel a call," he states to those who are about him, "and so I shall go now unto the Guardian. I request, EuDe'E, and the others of you who wish to journey with us, that we go unto the Guardian now."

Some of the brethren are so beautifully a part of the colors that they say unto our grouping, "We give to you the line-of-light and we shall remain here, for we are of a consciousness within that this is a good thing for we to do. Remember, we are ever with you, as sayeth thy Elder Brother."

As we come unto the Guardian, he smiles upon us with

the love of the Father and we return this.

He looketh upon EuDe'E, and we see Her smile, and he reaches out to embrace Her very gently, for he knoweth that She is yet (in a part of Her) focused upon the beauty of Her brethren, sisters and brothers who are yet in the No-Place Earth. Then, the Guardian steps back and looks upon Yo-El and all of us with that same love and sweetness.

"They have told me of you, sweet Guardian, and I know, within, the wonder of you and your choice to serve here. For this, I give to you my honor and my deep love, for I know that what you do has great purpose and meaning in accordance with our Brother, the Shining One's work ahead."

The Guardian smiles very warmly and looks upon Her with a certain knowing that we have seen in past, and he sayeth to Her, "Do you have awareness of your part in this?"

She glances from the Guardian to Yo-El and the rest of us. "I have some, but I believe that you know that my greatest ... shall I call it, love, lies in the feeling that I have for those who are yet not knowing this great freedom and love of the Father as we here do," and She turns to look upon us all.

We look at one another and smile, for we feel something different from Her.

Before anything else can be spoken, the Guardian sayeth, "A moment, please," and we perceive him not. Then we perceive him again and we are very joyful over this, for we have great love for this one, and the Guardian sayeth to EuDe'E, "I should like for you to know, now, in this time, these of my brethren ... only several who shall be with you in the times ahead, as there is that purpose and that need."

We look upon these that have returned with the Guardian in great wonder and awe, for they are likened unto he! Their beauty and magnificence is, indeed, like a light of the Father, shining through them and reflecting some beauty, some quality of such wonder from the Father. Yet, here they are. We look at one another and we look at Lom-Sa, who smiles one of his *Choose-a bit-of-the-quiet-thing* smiles. And so we do.

"These of my brethren," sayeth the Guardian, "will come to you in times ahead to give to you messages that, in those times, will have great meaning to you for the part that you shall play in the activities that are 'round and about the Shining One's future works. I am guided by the Father, that you shall know this, in this spirit-form of your being, that should you walk in another form, when that moment comes, you will know it to be true."

EuDe'E looks upon them. One comes forward and extends himself to Her, and She reaches out to become one with him.

Oh-h ... We feel such wondrous, majestic sounds, and the colors come dancing and go through us and bring us such a sense of rich love ... and peace that it is different, for we know it is not complete yet. We are joyful over this, for we know this is something from those colors at the edge of our Father's Word, which are going forth and creating in accordance with His Word.

We look to see if Yo-El or Lom-Sa would nod to us, but they do not, so we keep a bit of our quiet-thing in front of us. But we love this very dearly.

"I know these two," comments E-Ude to Yo-El. "They are of the Guardians. I have seen them in the places where the Father's Word has not manifest, not spoken, and it is pure and of our Father's sweetness."

Yo-El merely looks at him and nods, for he knows within that his brother speaks with love and truth. He looks back to see both of the other guardians, whom their dear Guardian has brought forth, becoming one with EuDe'E.

Then, after some experiences, they part.

EuDe'E turns to come to us all to be one with us,

without any energy of communication.

In our oneness, we become complete and we feel the wonder of these two new guardians to our knowing. We see the beauty of them. We see that they are a part of that which is to come, which the Shining One has spoken of to some portion, but this, we see, goes even further beyond this. We thank Her and give Her our love and completeness, for we know that She shall leave us, and we rejoice in this, for we know that it is good.

When we claim our uniqueness, She moves to become one with the guardians who are brothers to our Guardian. They begin to move. Suddenly, they are gone, but we know they have gone to be with the Shining One and the others and perhaps to be one with the Father.

We look to Yo-El and Lom-Sa, and it is Nov'A and the sisters who come forward to approach the Guardian.

He looks upon them and smiles, saying softly, "You feel it too, do you not?"

They answer, "We do,"

"Then rejoice in it, for thou knoweth that the Father calls to thee ... but in a time, as the Shining One has mentioned (by the measure of the No-Place Earth). That time is yet to come, but the knowing of it should bring you a sense of great wonder and joy. That, sweet sisters, is my prayer for you that I give to you now in this form." He gives unto them a beautiful array of colors and light.

They take it within and it seems to make them even more unique.

We look at one another and we think to ourselves, we would like this unique light and color. We look to the sisters and they smile upon us, and we become one and they share this with us and we feel the goodness of it.

But we hear the Guardian speaking to Yo-El and Lom-Sa and E-Ude and E-Am and the others, and we come back to listen as we feel the beauty of the maidens' energies, our sisters, flowing all throughout us.

"Several of your brethren have moved in groupings unto the No-Place Earth, using the pathways that you have so beautifully created."

Yo-El seems quite curious over this and asks, "How is it that we knew this not? Are we not one?"

The Guardian sayeth, "They wished to do this work in the same loving, joyful manner as has been done for Shem-of-God and these, thy brethren, and EuDe'E and all the others. They wished to do it so that all of you would see that they are truly one with you."

"What does this mean?" Yo-El asks very slowly and very carefully. "How is it possible that we are not one?"

The Guardian sayeth with equal softness and directness, "They have chosen to do this in a manner as a gift or blessing to all of you who have done this work that they were, at first, reluctant to be a part of. So they have gone with Dan-El and several groupings to show, in their own nature, that they and we are all one."

Yo-El is going into his contemplation-thing.

Several of our sisters go over to where he is, as does Lom-Sa and E-Ude and E-Am, and they become one. We decide to join them, so we become one with them to give them that which we are.

"I cannot find this in my knowing," Yo-El sayeth to Lom-Sa.

"Then you are not looking completely, my brother," sayeth Lom-Sa gently.

"Very well. Thank you." Yo-El does the contemplation-thing again, and then he smiles with the light of our Father's beauty. "I see it … rather in the same manner as our brethren moved off and created, at the onset, the No-Place, so have they chosen to do this in the manner of the gift-thing. But what need have we of gifts? We have all of the Father and each other, and every experience is filled with new discoveries and new gifts."

"No, it is not of the same nature," Lom-Sa states and turns to Il-Em with a smile.

Il-Em looks from Lom-Sa to Yo-El, and sayeth, "I know whereof he speaks. It is the nature of wanting to be, of themselves, something that perhaps was created in the Earth Place No-Place. It is called ..." He pauses to search for a way to communicate this to us, and then he speaks, "*Special.*"

We look at one another and we begin to laugh, for what little knowledge we have of this word from the No-Place Earth we see specialness everywhere, and are we not, each, special? We cannot grasp this but we listen very carefully from the quiet-place.

"It is something that has come forth from their work-things. They began their work-things as creations of beauty. You know, like our journeys into the colors and the many creations that come forth from our interaction together. And they began something that was of a nature that they tried to create better, each, than the other. Let me give you this knowing of it, for I do not know how to communicate it to you else than this."

Il-Em becomes one with Yo-El, and then all of us join in. We are in wonder of this, for, instead of becoming one and seeing the beauty of that which is the choices of the oneness, they are taking their individual uniqueness and trying to make it special unto itself in a very curious way.

We move about this knowing to look at it from different places, and it always looks the same ... very strange. So we put it in a thinking-place where we can come back and do the contemplation together and, perhaps, in that way, we can draw from it some understanding. So we turn back to listen.

Now the Guardian sayeth, "I will tell you this, as well, for I believe that soon you will have the knowing of it ...

that the journeys of thy brethren in the other groupings have not had the same outcome as those of your journeys, all of you together, previously."

"What is this, then?" sayeth E-Ude to the Guardian.

"I cannot give this to you, for I am here, in my choice, but I know it. I say to you, go to the Heaven Place and ask the Shining One's brethren, and they can tell you all of it."

We embrace the Guardian and thank him for his loving kindness and for the gifts he continually gives to us.

We become one and we look for one of the pathways.

We choose one, and, immediately, we are with the Shining One's brethren in the Heaven Place. A number of the Shining One's brethren come to us and we greet them in oneness with love and with our uniqueness, and they reciprocate this to us in return and many experiences are had by all of us.

Then, we listen as one of the guardians of this Heaven Place, in the name of the Shining One, comes over to us and sayeth this, "A curious thing has occurred. We can give you what we have in the knowing of it. Let us do that for you now."

So we become one and we become complete, and we do this very quickly because we wish the knowing of it, and we feel the experiences that this guardian of the Heaven Place knoweth. We say to him, "How is this possible? Have they forgotten our oneness, our lines-of-light? Have they forgotten the Sacred Places?"

He sayeth, "No, but they are …" He pauses for a moment and we know that he is looking for a pathway to give us that information that we will have understanding, and he does.

Oh-h … We are in such wonder of this! We thank this one who, among the others of the Shining One's brethren, are now guardians of the Heaven Place, and we move back into the Father's Word that we can feel the purity of this and the love and joy that is constantly flowing and in the alive-thing, and not in the not-alive-thing of the No-Place Earth.

"It is part of that death-thing they have created," one of our brothers sayeth to us.

We look upon him and we remember it from the knowing-place.

Yo-El and a number of our brethren are clearly not understanding what has transpired, even after the contemplation of it. So, Yo-El sayeth to us with joy, "Let us become one. Let us place our uniqueness together and let us go to the Sacred Place and bring this forth, and, this time, let us call our Father."

We do. Oh-h, we so love the peace and joy of this oneness as we call the Father. We feel such magnificence of color and light and blessings of all forms, some we have no names for.

> Then, we hear,
> *I give you my love, my sweet Children.*
> *Dost thou call me?*

We laugh because we know the Father knoweth we called Him because He has come, and we find great joy in this, as does He. We laugh together and sing songs and dance dances, and we have many experiences like this. We always feel so very complete and wonderful in our uniqueness and in our oneness as we do this with the Father. It is so wonderful.

Then, there comes the experience where Yo-El sayeth, "We do not understand this thing that our brethren have done, and in several groupings."

> The Father looks upon him and moves close to Yo-El and sayeth,
> *Where is your understanding, if you do not*

understand this?

Yo-El looks upon the Father and begins to smile, "Thank You, my Father." He pauses for a moment, and then he returns to us with such a brilliance!

"Oh! Is it Yo-El? Or is it the Shining One?"

E-Ude begins to laugh softly as he looks upon us and we understand that our thinking-things have been of more humor here as we have learned to do them.

"I would like to help my brethren if they are somehow unable to free themselves and their brethren whom they had gone to retrieve from the No-Place Earth. I have the knowing of it now, Father. But, why did they choose to do the things that our brethren of the No-Place were doing? Why did they ..."

The Father touches him and smiles, and Yo-El, we see, grows brighter. Lom-Sa and E-Ude and Il-Em and all of them grow very bright, and come together in oneness with the Father. We look upon one another, and we laugh and decide to become one with them, too, so then we knoweth this and we have the knowing as Yo-El has called forth.

We dwell with the Father for a time.

Then He calls forth the Sacred Place within each of us and gives it His love, and, then, He tells us to be about our experiences, as we choose them. There is something that He gives to our brothers and sisters, and we know that we shall know this so we stay in the gifts He has given us, and the Father is gone, with a sprinkling of His laughter and love.

The Shining One sayeth to EuDe'E, "The Guardian has shown you?"

"Yes," She smiles. "I have some knowing of it, but he, himself, has said that the greater knowing lies ahead and that it will come when its experience is ready. So, these two beautiful guardians have brought me here to be in the

Oneness with you and the Father. We shall do a beautiful work together, or more than one *work* (as they call it in the Earth), and it will have to do with the Earth, itself. Yes?"

The Shining One responds, "Yes, my sweet Sister."

AoLe'A comes close to Her and embraces Her, and then many of the other of the Shining One's brethren come and become one with them all.

"What of my brethren who are yet in the Earth in this time, as they measure it?"

The Shining One sayeth, "They are moving, with their time, very quickly and they are creating many experiences. Though it may seem, not to the knowing of it, not to the understanding of it, they are seeking to make themselves even more separate, as curious as that might sound to you."

EuDe'E shakes Her consciousness back and forth like a head-thing, and gives a laugh, for it is a reflection of her previous journey in the No-Place Earth, and they all laugh. "It is a curious thing that has ..." She pauses for a moment and reaches within and then brings forth this, "It is like a curious consciousness that moves all about the No-Place Earth, and those who are a part of it support it, and give it energy and strive to overpower or convince others of our brethren, that the energy might grow stronger. It was very strong when our brethren came and set us free. Now, I have a feeling, within, that the calls of my sisters and brothers might not even be heard because of the covering and the No-Place energy-thing."

The Shining One comes to Her, very closely, and smiles upon Her, and the love and light of His smile seems to bring Her peace, as it might be that the Father gives peace. "All will be well, my sweet Sister. All will be well. But it is their right to choose and the right of the brethren who are ... shall we call this *lost*?"

She sayeth, "No, not lost."

"What then?" the Shining One responds smilingly.

"They have lost their way."

The Shining One nods upon this thing and sees it as good. So He sayeth, "Yes, they have lost their way. We have brethren who are seeking to bring the way to them."

EuDe'E sayeth, much to the wonder of all there present, "Yes, and I feel, within, that they will struggle with the energy, the power of the No-Place Earth. Will they find the way?"

The Shining One looks deep within Her and becomes one with Her, as does AoLe'A.

All of the Shining One's brethren gather together in oneness and move closer and closer to the Father, and He reaches out to embrace them. The guardians remain, giving their loving energy to the present preservation of the wonder of the All.

"Much has changed, then," Yo-El sayeth. "They move their time-thing very quickly, I feel, and our brethren who have gone, in the other groupings, may not have had the knowing of this because they sought to do this without the oneness and the completeness. Too much of this was done in and of their own uniqueness and without ... Well, you understand, my brethren."

We do. We look upon this with Yo-El and all the others very curiously for a time. We put it in the center of our oneness, this special-thing, and we continue to look at it.

Lom-Sa sayeth to us, "This is good, for, as one seeks to move into oneness with a thing or to bring it your completeness, it is good to know it. In this instance, it does not wish our oneness or our completeness; it wishes, rather, in its terms, to be special. Their specialness has grown and grown, as I find on the path within me, to where they now have formed a challenge to one another for the greatest specialness, and this challenge seems to be gaining power very quickly.

"Many, many of them have gathered into groupings to energize their challenge to overcome the challenges of others. It is, indeed, not likely that any of these would consider oneness with us. They place their uniqueness into a challenge-form of uniqueness that it can do this (as they call it) competition-thing with one another's challenges. It is a complex and curious mechanism, but it is growing in its power in the No-Place Earth."

One of our brothers comes forward and asks him, "How do they build this challenge-thing, or any of it, without the Father?"

Lom-Sa sayeth, "It is the presence of the Father and those of the element that are gathered by them there, in the No-Place Earth, but it is not in the completeness. They recognize the Father in a curious way ... as very distant, and in many different forms that are also not agreed upon."

Yo-El sayeth softly, "Thank you, all of you ... and you, Lom-Sa. Now I ask of you, and I put this forward in the center of our grouping, how are we to set them free again? How can we bring them the pathway?"

We do many contemplations on this. We go to the Memory Place and bring out the living pathways that we have used in past, and we see these past pathways as having been covered with some of their No-Place Earth fragments. We look at one another and sayeth this, "Yo-El, let us become one and bring our completeness into the Sacred Places within, that we might call the Father, for our contemplations tell us very little. We have naught knowing of this. How can we gather the knowing of it when they do not permit this?"

"We would need to ..." and the one who is speaking looks this way and that, and so we speak, together, with him. "We would need to violate that which the Father sayeth we cannot violate. We really need to talk to our Father!"

We begin to laugh with joy and we celebrate and dance and sing songs, for, in the knowing of this, we are free. We place it as a thing in the center of our grouping, and, in our oneness, we call the Father.

The Father sayeth to us gently,
Look you, my Children ... You have done many experiences, have you not?

He laughs and we laugh with Him and we become one, and we do the dancing and celebrating-things.

Then the Father sayeth,
My word is My word, Children, and that is so. You cannot violate their right of choice.

"Well, Father," sayeth one, "look at this thing ... We have placed it in the center. How can we know it? It won't let us be one with it. We can't bring it our uniqueness. It's just ... Well, it's not very friendly, Father."

We all laugh very, very much about this new word ... the *friendly*-word.

The Father sayeth to us in the same humor,
Well, are you being friendly with it?

We look to our brother who spoke this to the Father, and we laugh and he laughs with us.

"Well, no, Father. I suppose I am not being very friendly with it. But, how can I be friendly with it?" He walks about the thing and he reaches to touch it, and it moves away from his touch. He looks to the Father and he sayeth, "See, Father? It doesn't want to be friendly with me."

The Father sayeth,
Be in your uniqueness, my son.

He does.

Now, bring your uniqueness to the thing, as you call it. And do not touch it, but embrace it with your uniqueness all about without touching it.

So our brother does this.

We look to one another and we smile and say, "He doeth this thing very well," and we look back quickly.

Our brother is embracing the thing with his uniqueness, and the thing is just being still.

See? the Father sayeth.

The thing has a way of seeing you as not being friendly to it.

If you can take your uniqueness and simply place it about that thing and let it be just as an offering, then the thing can't push on you like it did, because you are not pushing on it.

The brother, who we see as very, very bright in the contemplation-thing, sayeth to our Father very quickly, "But I merely touched it, Father. I didn't strive to push it."

The Father laughs mightily.

Take this into your contemplation and see the truth in it: If you offer it your uniqueness and that alone, how can it have any response to you?

The brother looks at the Father and looks at the thing covered with his uniqueness, and he sayeth to the Father, "I wish to be one with You, Father. This thing is not coming into knowing very easily."

The Father laughs very heartily and scoops up our brother and all of us with Him, and we go soaring about in our Father's Word, giving off beautiful lights and colors and gifts and blessings to all of our brethren whom we meet who quickly join with us.

Then, we come to a pause in an experience.

The Father sayeth,
*Look upon these things as you have learned from
them. You contemplate going to the No-Place Earth to
help the groupings of your brethren who have gone
without your oneness into the No-Place to do a good
work, to answer calls. Where have they made a wrong
choice that has caused them to lose their way?*

Yo-El, who has been watching and laughing and being
joyful with this, these gifts from the Father, sayeth, "I think
I may feel it within, Father. For in my experiences there, I
see something from the nature of our brethren in the Earth
who seek ..." and he pauses for a moment to choose
carefully his communication to the Father, "to seek
dominance over others."

The Father laughs.
*Oh, you have another word-thing that you have
created.*

Yo-El laughs mightily, and sayeth, "No, I have gathered
it from them. I have only given life to it and freedom to it."

The Father goeth to him and embraces him,
and states,
Well spoken, my brothers. Well spoken, my son.

We are all joyful for this from the Father. It is a very
beautiful thing, for, as the Father recognizes this in Yo-El,
it is a gift to all of us.

So our experience continues.

Then the Father departs from us, that we might pursue
our experiences and our knowing of these things that have
been brought from contemplation and given expression.

And so we do.

There is a curious thing that we find, as we are in our
oneness ... Somehow we do not feel the wonder of our

completeness to the degree that we have in past, and we look to Lom-Sa.

He sayeth, "It is that which you have naught, that you feel as a part of the lack you are experiencing in the present."

We look upon this and contemplate it and we know that he refers to our brethren who have lost their way in the Earth and we turn to Yo-El and say to him, "What are we to do about this?"

Yo-El sayeth, "This is not a truth." He turns to Lom-Sa and asks of him, "What you have given to my brethren and I is something that we do not need to claim, in the manner as those who seek to dominate in the Earth claim things to make them their own."

Lom-Sa studies Yo-El very carefully and nods, encouraging him to go on.

"I never feel a sense of anything but perfect completion and oneness within me. I have the knowing of it, sweet Lom-Sa, but I have no less than completeness. What they do and what they are about is their choice. I do not choose as they choose. Therefore, I am complete, am I not?" and he turns to all of us and sayeth, "as are they."

Lom-Sa smiles very, very brightly and goeth to Yo-El and stands before him. "Then you have that, as you sayeth it for, if you say it and know it, then it is yours. I have given these things in response to our brethren here, that there might come forth from you the knowing of that which is righteousness and truth. If you can, here, before me now, say that you are, in truth, complete and that there is naught within you that is lacking, even as thou knoweth thy brethren to have lost their way in the No-Place, then ... Well, you have made a wondrous discovery and I encourage you to make it your own even moreso."

Yo-El looks upon him with great compassion and love for this one he loves very dearly, and Lom-Sa knoweth this.

Then, Nov'A and the sisters, E-Am and Il-Em and
E-Ude, all come to gather with them very closely. We have a
sense of honoring them in what they do, so we make a quiet
place and surround them in this quiet-place.

Yo-El is moving in a way that is very beautiful. It is an
inner moving-thing and we see that it is doing something to
his uniqueness. We look within ourselves to see our
uniqueness, and we think, perhaps, we shall do this
moving-thing to our uniqueness, too. But for now we shall
stay in the quiet-thing.

Then, the others ... Nov'A, Cel'A, the third sister, E-
Am, Il-Em, E-Ude, and a number of the others very, very
close to them ... all make this change in their uniqueness,
this movement of their uniqueness that grows brighter, and
we look at one another, but we keep the quiet-thing.

Lom-Sa sayeth, then, to all of them, and turns to look
upon us that he knoweth that we seek this, too, "What the
Father has given to each of us, in our uniqueness, has also
the Word, the very Breath of the Father, within it. And the
more you go within your uniqueness and find that which is
of the Father as His gift of Righteousness, and all else, then
the moreso does your uniqueness become as a reflection of
our Father.

We are in wonder of this as Lom-Sa has stated this.
Why, this is as the Shining One! We look at our uniqueness
to see, "Is there that of the Shining One in *our*
uniqueness?" We look very carefully at each and another's
uniqueness, and we see a bit of it! We are so joyful we
begin to sing, and, as we are surrounding them, our song
and our dance and our laughter and our joy fills them with
the same.

We go spiraling off into the Word of our Father, and
we all reach out to touch the brilliance of Yo-El 's shining

in his uniqueness and we find it very, very good.

We soar off to the periphery of the colors and we see them calling out to them, and we call out to them and we move into our uniqueness and go and dance among the colors. We laugh and sing songs and we feel the beauty of the colors coming and sharing with one another in us. And we feel so good. Then we feel it within our uniqueness, and we look at one another and sayeth, "Our uniqueness is very much like our Sacred Places. Could it be they are the same?"

But before we can contemplate on this, we hear the Guardian's call, and we move into oneness.

Instantly, we are with the Guardian.

He looks upon us all, and he smiles upon Yo-El and Lom-Sa, and sayeth to Lom-Sa, "You are growing in your wisdom-thing, for you have seen into the No-Place and seen into the energies there and have understood them from your own uniqueness. I see you have done, with this wisdom, a very good work."

Lom-Sa merely nods and smiles the light of love to him.

We marvel at Lom-Sa and now we see that he too is changing in his uniqueness, and we celebrate this inwardly, but we keep the outer quiet so that we can listen.

The Guardian has moved very close to Yo-El, and the others with him. "I see you contemplate how you might make the way open and passable for your brethren to be freed from the No-Place Earth."

Yo-El merely smiles and nods to the Guardian.

"Doing what Lom-Sa has helped you bring forth would serve you well, for know this ... The power of their uniqueness, while it might not be in oneness with you and your brethren, is still that of Child of God."

"I believe I understand," sayeth Yo-El.

"Then it is good," sayeth the Guardian, "for you will need this understanding and all that you can bring into the light of your uniqueness for your journey."

"What has happened?" the brethren sayeth unto Dan-El.

"We have not followed the pathway in the same truth and honor as our brethren before us have done, and we have not let the Oneness nourish us as they have done," sayeth Dan-El.

"But, then, we must do this now, for they cover us more and more by the measure of passing of their time."

Dan-El sayeth, "This I know, my brothers. But let us now do what we can for those whom we have come to set free."

"And what is that?" sayeth this one to Dan-El.

"We give to them that which we have to give, and together we can build our Oneness again."

"Even under this covering?" he sayeth.

"I believe this. If you believe it and we all believe it and we make it that which we are, then they will hear our call and we shall make it mighty and bright."

Before they can comment further, a great force from the No-Place Earth that is their intent darkens them even more.

15

Pledge to the Living Promise

Yo-El has gathered up, according to their will and choice, a goodly number of his brethren and has called them into oneness, that they might go unto the Sacred Symbol and look upon the pathways (as they have come to know them) and to seek the wisdom as is now growing within Lom-Sa, that they might know that which is of the greater choice to proceed unto the works. They feel and know the presence of the guardians of the Shining One from the Heaven Place offering to them their knowing and their blessing.

Their contemplation moves into the realization that much has grown and changed upon the Earth No-Place and that, even so as their brethren are, in a manner of speaking, bound unto that realm of expression as it is now come to be known, it is only that which they see and accept that can bind them.

In the truth of this knowing, Yo-El calls forth Lom-Sa, "Show us that path which is aright, that we ..." pointing to several of his companions, "may follow unto that which will give us the understanding of the opportunities before us."

Lom-Sa brings forth the light of his uniqueness, and we all gather around this and give unto it our uniqueness, called forth from the Sacred Place within.

We move with ease, passing through the Heaven Place, greeting the guardians who are yet here, and acknowledging that they are with us in this good work, and gently, moving through the elements and through the expressions and works that we see are now, for the most part, in place in those defined areas between the realms (as shall come to be known in the later days), according to their wishes.

We pass through the River of Light with such a joy and wonder, and we feel, ever, the Father's great blessings unto all of us and unto the Earth No-Place.

We come into the energies of the mind-thing. We look upon these and see that they have gathered some knowing unto themselves and that many energies of curious nature move about upon the mind-thing. We claim the pathway of passage in our true nature, as children of God, and we move with ease through this, and behold the beauty and wonder of the creations that are now present in the Earth No-Place.

We move very near the expressions upon the surface of the Earth No-Place, looking upon them and seeing that many of our brethren of the No-Place Earth are tending them, and we see, within the presence of their tending, a certain beautiful light that calls into a remembrance of how much we love them.

With ease and wonder, as we pass near to them, we see that they know us not, nor do they perceive our presence, and we thank Lom-Sa for his choice of this beautiful pathway.

We come near unto where we can determine that our brethren of the first grouping are likely to be located, and we see a very large glowing amassing of the mind-energy-thing. And we are in wonder of this!

Yo-El sayeth, "Look, you … It is not the particles of the elements, but something else that they have called to bind our brethren, in such a way as their light cannot reach to oneness."

Nov'A and Cel'A and the third sister come forward, and we look upon them as they reach out to know this. We see them react to it, seeing the energies of it as though it were a grouping of our brethren, rather than an energy-thing.

Yo-El calleth the sisters back unto our oneness, and we contemplate this in the Sacred Place that is called forth from within our uniqueness. "It is as the guardian of the Heaven Place has stated to us, that much time has passed by and many things, as they measure it, have been known and gathered up."

Il-Em sayeth unto Yo-El, "It is their order of things. It is, of some beautiful measure (by the nature as we knoweth this), that they have created a pathway of their movement of their time's evolution and of the mind-thing, and much more that I know not."

Yo-El sayeth unto Lom-Sa, "Let us call forth the lines-of-light and seek from our brother, Shem."

So, we come together in a joyful celebration of oneness, placing that which is Sacred from within each of us into the center of our grouping. But we do not call the Father. Rather, we seek the beautiful lines-of-light that are ever present with us in our oneness. Once again, to our delight and wonder, we look upon them.

There is a glowing energy and a beautiful light, within the center of which we can discern the image of Shem, once again.

The sisters move, as in past, to surround him and they move gently about him. We can feel their love for him as he gives to them in return.

"You have followed a pathway to the Earth No-Place."

"Yes," responds Yo-El, with a gentleness and understanding of the wisdom of Shem that can be felt by all of us.

We look upon one another and we think, "How is it that he has this?" And we think to ourselves, "We should like to have this."

Lom-Sa looks upon us carefully, and we reach within to pull forth the quiet-thing, and we do this very well. But still, we place this question in our Knowing Place, that we might contemplate it later.

"It is as might be anticipated," begins Shem gently, the light about him moving and shifting with such brilliance.

Oh, we long to go and be one with him.

Then Lom-Sa looks with loving intent at us, and we bring forth the quiet-thing very carefully, so as not to think beyond it.

"It is good," continues Shem, "to recognize that, because they have chosen their presence in what has come to be known as the Earth No-Place, they continue with their growth of awareness. In other words, just as we have made many new, wondrous experiences, they, as well, draw upon that oneness with the Father and they, too, in a manner of speaking, are growing in their experiences, as well."

"What, then, is this that we perceive upon our brethren … this mind-thing's energy? It is different than the element fragments that they used in past."

"Indeed," comments Shem very softly and very gently, as though it were something that troubled him to speak it. "It is that they have recognized that there is greater than what is found in the movement of the elements; that they, within themselves, can bring together what they call their thought-things and their exercise of mind. What you perceive is the result of all of these experiences that they have come to know. It is, in and of itself, of no-thing as you think of the Earth-Place. But in the presence of the creations and that which they have builded, it has a certain state of being."

"Can you explain to us," questions Yo-El, "what this state of being is?"

"I have not known it to the depth and breadth of that which I am perceiving through you. But I believe that they draw from the same source, as do all of we … that it is the uniqueness of their oneness with the Father. Though they see Him as distant, they claim somewhat (as you can see) the *power* of the Father."

We look upon the energy of the mind-thing and we see it moving. We think of some of the work-things that they have builded and given life to, and we begin to understand this. "Have you a guidance for us, dear Shem, on how we might encounter our brethren, and help them to know themselves in their completeness and be one with us?'"

Shem pauses for a time, and we can see that somewhere within his being he is seeking the answers for us, and we are very excited about this. We want to sing and dance about it, but Shem-El waggles himself at us in a curious way that brings us humor (but, quiet humor).

Shem begins, rather slowly at first, "It is not that I have the direct knowing of this, but what I am perceiving is that they will likely know of your presence in a manner that is different for you. But if you remember that you are one with them and honor them and honor yourself, I should think that the way will be open for you, but in the nature of this, it is not truly known for it is in the realm of their free will."

"I thank you, dear Shem," comments Yo-El, softly. "It is, within me, a call that they cannot be that distant. They must still know we are brethren."

Shem only smiles and gives a light of his oneness to Yo-El.

He reciprocates.

Then, the light comes into brilliance and the sisters begin to move again, in another way, and Shem is gone.

There is a curious feeling in us, for we have great love for him and we feel from him something that is very close to our Father, but unique.

Il-Em, E-Ude, E-Am are in contemplation. They are in contemplation and they look upon this, as has been given, and Lom-Sa and the sisters move into the contemplation-thing.

Then, rather than our joining into oneness, they move from this very swiftly.

Yo-El sayeth, "Let me choose this pathway and move to the No-Place, and feel this in the uniqueness of my being and in my oneness with thee. And, as there is the knowing within you, do as you know to do. And all is well, for we here are in oneness, and we shall hold this all throughout."

He looketh upon us, and we claim that oneness and we knoweth it to be true and good. We build the sacredness of the Symbol and the pathway within it, and our oneness becomes very, very beautiful, and we feel the love of the Father moving all throughout.

It is upon the pathway of this, our Father's love, that Yo-El moves very gently with the sisters and Il-Em unto the No-Place Earth.

We keep our line of light with them and we feel and know as they do, and we are grateful for this. At first we are smitten in our Joy Place with the beauty that we perceive through them.

Yo-El looks about and sayeth to the sisters, "Indeed, these are our brethren. Look you, how they have brought aspects of the elements and given their uniqueness to them. Very, very beautiful. Yet, there is something curious here."

Nov'A comes close to him and sayeth, "It is the not-free-thing."

Il-Em looks at her curiously and looks about, and then, from within his Sacred Place, he discerns this and then returns and sayeth to her, "Thank you, sister, I have knowing of it now. Thank you."

Nov'A moves back to her position, and Yo-El and Il-Em move forward and they come very near to the energy of the mind-thing.

To our surprise, Yo-El sayeth to the mind-thing, "Peace be with you."

The mind-thing seems to hear this! We ponder how it does because we can only see the energy of it, not the uniqueness of it.

Then, to our wonder, a voice speaks to Yo-El, "What seek you here?"

"I have come to be one with my brethren, whom I

believe are within your being,"

The mind-thing begins to move about, and we see the energies and all sorts of things within it.

Then, we see the sisters beginning to move, and we look about and we see brethren of the Earth No-Place coming very swiftly!

Yo-El turns to confront them, to our wonder, again, and sayeth to them, "I greet you, my brethren."

One comes to the forefront and moves very close to Yo-El and sayeth, "What do you seek here? This is not for you to be here."

Yo-El sayeth to him, "I seek only oneness with my brothers and sisters who have come here for the goodness of those they seek."

"We have not called you, nor are you welcome here. If you do not depart, we shall claim you here."

Yo-El looks at him very carefully, and we see him do something very beautiful ... He extends to him a portion of his uniqueness.

The entity looketh upon this, and we can see that it is having an impact upon him. He begins to move this way and that and he turns to his brethren and then back to Yo-El. "I know this, and I know that it is not to be bound here. But I say to you neither have you the right here."

"I have the right of freedom."

The entity begins to laugh very loudly, and the others with him begin to echo. "The freedom here, as you say this, is by the choice of those who are here, not by your choice."

"I seek not to disrupt that which is yours, nor your choice, but I say again to you, I shall now join my brethren and I should like you to part your mind-thing, else I shall part it in the Name of our Father."

They look at one another somewhat with humor, and somewhat with a curious force or energy we know not.

He turns back to Yo-El, "We do not see your Father

here. How is He to help you?

Yo-El says not another Word, but turns, and he and Il-Em walk straight away into the mind-thing, and, to the awe of the challenging brethren, they disappear within it.

There is a shimmering that passes through the mind-thing and then it quiets itself to what it was previously.

Yo-El and Il-Em are in their oneness and we can, through the knowing of them, follow our line-of-light which has no reckoning with the mind-thing, for it disturbs it not. Neither does it allow it any quarter in its purity.

Some of our brethren gasp at the appearance of Yo-El and Il-Em, and some of them fall unto the No-Place Earth as though they are doing that weeping-thing. But we know it is their joy and their wonder. We can see that it was their belief that they were to be *forever* in the No-Place Earth (as the No-Place Earth measures it) and perhaps even that no-life-thing would be theirs to experience.

"Look you," sayeth Il-Em. "It is not that they have used their mind-thing to get you to believe; it is that you are not of this Place and that your oneness with us cannot be obscured or in any way limited by any force. For our oneness is of the Father."

The more Il-Em speaks, the more do these, our brethren, brighten, and the mind-thing begins to expand, moving out from them more and more.

"Where are those whose call you have come to answer?" asks Yo-El softly.

Dan-El looks up from his previous thankfulness place and sayeth to Yo-El, "They are there. See? Where the mind-thing grows very, very thick, they are within there. We cannot view them anymore. We have tried to serve them, but the mind-thing has claimed them."

Again, Yo-El looks upon Il-Em and sayeth to Dan-El thereafter, "Claim your oneness and brighten your brethren, my brothers and sisters, and know this thing to be of the Earth No-Place, not of our oneness and your uniqueness. Know it and claim it. Do it, *now*."

Then, Yo-El and Il-Em turn and walk straight away, right up to the thickening of the mind-thing, and we hear him say, "In the peace of our Father's love cometh we to answer a call in the Name of our Father. We seek naught from you, nor do we seek to take from you. But it is, in the nature of our oneness, righteous that we come to answer a call. The call cannot be limited, for they are Children of God, as are those who have created you and who give you life. Now, you may part or we shall pass through you, and as we do, we shall give of the Father's love to you. And we know that it shall awaken that which is in the mind of those who have created you. You are our brethren."

The mind-thing quivers and shakes. Then come lights and beautiful energies ... We wonder where they came from, and then we look at each other and smile, for certainly they have come from our brethren.

Without hesitation, Yo-El and Il-Em move into the mind-thing, and it parts for them! Oh, we are so joyful! We look at one another and we acknowledge our joy and we try to keep it very, very ... Well, we look at Lom-Sa and he nods and smiles, and we keep it in the quiet-place. (But we can see that our joy is creating beautiful lights of energy upon the unification of our sacred uniqueness, and we think that this is good.)

Yo-El and Il-Em look about this way and that, for, even though they have passed through the mind-thing, there is a dullness here, something they have not known. Yet, they hold their oneness together. They move through the mind-thing, the grayness of it, but they keep their light of love from the Father in some moderation so as to honor the mind-thing of their brethren whom they know are knowing this.

Suddenly, Yo-El feels something in his Sacred Place

and then does Il-Em. They look upon one another and they move very completely into oneness, and they hear a sweet voice saying to them, "Thank you, my brothers, for answering the call of my sisters and brothers, that I might know them here in oneness with my brethren." And they know it is EuDe'E.

They look upon one another's uniqueness with such joy, that they could be of service to Her. They reach within without another contemplation and find the Sacred Place, each of them, and they touch the Mark of the Shining One and they feel His sweetness and His pure love, as though it were the Father who giveth this. And they are renewed.

The gray substance of the mind-thing moves away from this beautiful light, and now they see the sisters and brothers that She has spoken of.

They go to them, and they see that they are in varying states of awareness of their presence.

Yo-El chooses one off to the side who seems to be in a contemplation-thing. He moves to her level and slowly allows a sound of oneness to come from himself to her. Her contemplation brightens, and Il-Em moves to the other side of her and lets his unique sound of oneness gently come forth, and she brightens more. Soon, she looks upon them, and we feel her joy as though someone were being born into the wonder of our Father's Word once again.

Oh, we are so joyful, and we feel such a love for her! We move to our Sacred Places in the center of our oneness and we give thanks to the Father. We are so very thankful.

Yo-El reaches out to her and she accepts him, and slowly ... very, very slowly, as though Yo-El were recognizing those Limiting Forces that have placed themselves in dominion over her, Yo-El blesses them to leave her. In the Mark of our Shining One Brother they move away, for they seek not His Mark, nor the light of it.

We see Il-Em moving to another and another, and

Yo-El and this awakened sister do the same. Soon there are many of them, and they brighten.

The darkened mind-thing has moved off from them, and there are Dan-El and the other brothers and sisters. We see them, with celebratory oneness, moving into oneness.

Then the mind-thing parts very broadly, and there are the brethren of the Earth again and the challenger! "What is it that you are seeking to do?"

Yo-El sayeth to him, "I seek only that which is the right of these, our brethren, to choose."

"You cannot, for they *have* chosen, and they are here and they are within the embrace of the No-Place Law."

Yo-El turns to Il-Em and Il-Em gives him an affirmation. They become one, and Yo-El sayeth from their oneness, "Look you, brother. Here is my uniqueness and that of my brother."

The challenger shields himself from seeing this and begins to back away, and those of the great number who are with him do the same, moving off into the work-things ... their creations and such.

In that moment, the sisters move to closeness to all of these and begin their dance and their song, and we move, with strength, to the center of this pathway in our uniqueness. We hold the wonder of our uniqueness in our Father's Name, holding love for all of our brethren in the No-Place Earth.

Yo-El sayeth to them, "Move, you. Now! Go along this pathway. Here, Dan-El ... Lead them."

They follow Dan-El and his grouping to be in our midst, and we are joyful and celebratory with such completeness. Then, one in our grouping sayeth, "What of Yo-El and Il-Em?"

We pause to look back along the Line-of-Light and we see that they are, yet, as they were.

The challenger begins to move closer to them.

Yo-El sayeth very gently, "Where are the others who have called out?"

The challenger begins to do his word-thing and many other of his mind-things are hurtled at our brethren, but they merely fall to the No-Place Earth, for they cannot pass through the light of our brethren.

Yo-El realizes that the challenger will not give this, and so we feel, along the line-of-light, that Yo-El and Il-Em ask Lom-Sa to look upon the No-Place Earth to discern where they might find them, and we place all of our brethren in the center of our sacredness and focus upon this.

Lom-Sa moves into a very beautiful contemplation and we give him our light of the Father's love, and very quickly he sayeth, "They are near to the water-thing. Here, go you here," and he gives this to our brothers.

Yo-El looks a moment at the challenger and those with him, and sayeth, "We love you. We wish you well," and they move very swiftly along the pathway.

We see our brethren of the Earth No-Place doing the angry-thing, but they cannot make any limitation to our brothers.

Again, we see Yo-El and Il-Em move to another shimmering mind-thing mass. This time, it is as though the mind-thing knows the events that occurred in the other mind-things. So, they enter it with rapidity and ease, to our wonder, and there are more of our brethren from the other grouping who have journeyed along the pathway to answer calls. Again, they repeat the gentle, loving process of calling them forth to know themselves and to know their uniqueness.

The sisters have positioned themselves around the periphery, and we see them begin to shimmer with light and move about, as we see others of the brethren of the Earth No-Place coming to see what has disrupted their mind-thing mass.

This time the sisters make a joyful song and dance, and the brethren of the Earth No-Place pause on the distance from the presence of our sisters' dance. The distance is goodly. We look in wonder, for the sisters' dance curiously seems to touch them in a way that we think might call forth their uniqueness. It does not, but it seems to place them in the energy of a different intent. The strength and force of their previous hostility of intent is greatly moderated and they seem to even be moving a bit to and fro to the beauty of our sisters' dance, and then we know that the oneness of our sisters touches them near the Sacred Place.

We look at one another in a great wonder of this and we say, "Let us take this to the Knowing Place, that we can ask the Father about it in a later contemplation."

Lom-Sa smiles and nods upon us and thanks us for doing the quiet-thing so well.

Yo-El and Il-Em are very busied, calling to consciousness the uniqueness of our brethren, and it seems that the mind-thing has had an even greater impact upon them. We feel the call from Yo-El, and we give more of our uniqueness and our light of the Father's love to them along the line-of-light, the oneness. We see them brighten with this, and they continue to call forth the uniqueness again and again.

Then, to our wonder, Nov'A begins to slow her dance and moves within the mind-thing and places her uniqueness around Yo-El and our brother, Il-Em! Very swiftly, she calls to us to make the oneness stronger, and so we do. To our wonder, E-Am and E-Ude move along the path of light into the mind-thing to be with our brothers and Nov'A, that they can add the beauty of their uniqueness to the work that they are seeking to undo that has been done upon our brethren.

With a light of joy, Nov'A moves back to our sisters and

resumes her dance. It is good because some of our brethren of the No-Place begin to advance in that area where Nov'A had departed. Her dance brightens, and they move back a ways.

Then we hear Il-Em say to Yo-El, "I think it not possible, my brother, that we can seek out all those who may have called, for their call cannot be discerned. Even at the depth of my uniqueness I do not perceive them."

Yo-El pauses and we see him move into his own uniqueness and to the Sacred Place within, and he summons the Mark of our Brother and they are one in this.

Then, after a time of contemplation, Yo-El comes back from his Sacred Place and sayeth to Il-Em, "It is in my knowing that you are correct. Let us do what we can and bring these to their uniqueness and our oneness with them, for I perceive that the mind-thing is growing again. Let us move now back to our grouping in the Sacred Symbol."

They gather up all of them. Not a one is left behind, of their knowing.

They move without the mind-thing and the sisters surround them, and instantly they are here, and we feel a rush of something that we have not known. It is a joy, yes, that our brethren are returned and free. But, something else ...

Lom-Sa sayeth to us, "Quickly now, place it into your Knowing Place that we might later contemplate it. Let us strengthen our oneness and call forth the Sacred uniqueness and surround us with that."

We feel this in a curious way ... Something from the Earth No-Place wants us to be with it.

Lom-Sa sayeth, "Look, you, to the center in our Sacred uniqueness. Now! Let us move to the Heaven Place!"

We feel the movement ... slower at first, but then

gaining a rapidity. As we pass through the River of Light, it is as though we are all refreshed with the joy of the colors, and we soar swiftly to the Heaven Place.

We greet the guardians and they surround us, and we move to the center of our Father's Word.

We come to a place of pause and we look upon one another. We look to Lom-Sa and all our brethren, and they are all so bright and so joyful and we feel the excitement of their energy.

Yet, we look ... We search for Yo-El and Il-Em. We come upon them and we look upon them with wonder, for they are somehow different.

So, we call for oneness and our brethren from the No-Place Earth joyfully move into oneness with us. We celebrate only briefly, and we call forth the Sacredness from within each of us and it is complete.

And we call, "Father ..."

We feel something, and we sayeth again, "Father, we call You."

Then, in the center of our grouping, we can perceive the Father's light. It grows, and then we feel His love for us.

We rush to embrace Him and He embraces us. Then, after these experiences, we say to Him, "Father, look You at these good works that have been done. Our brothers and sisters, who are now in Your Sacred Word ... their freedom is complete. Their uniqueness shineth again."

The Father looks upon them and touches each one. We feel the love between them, and the experience moves.

Then, we ask the Father, "Look, Father. Here are Yo-El and Il-Em."

Yo-El and Il-Em joyfully greet the Father.

The Father does not embrace them yet, but looks upon them.

You have had a good journey, have you not, my sons?

The sisters move to surround them.

The Father sayeth to them in the light of the sisters,

You have given of your uniqueness to that which is called the work, in the No-Place Earth. It is, my sweet sons, something that you have come into knowing: that when you seek such a work, it is very, very good for you to remember that we are one; and that, when you doeth a work as you have, in My love and in My presence, doeth it in oneness with Me ... not of yourselves, alone.

Yo-El looks to Il-Em, and Il-Em at he, and they begin to laugh very softly at first, and then they rush to the Father and embrace Him.

The sisters surround them and embrace the Father with them, and we all rush to embrace the Father in a great oneness.

We do the great dance and song of oneness all throughout the Father's Word. We move off to celebrate and give gifts to the colors and to receive blessings from them, and we give these to our newly awakened brothers and sisters and they give to us in return. It is very, very good.

Then Yo-El cometh to Lom-Sa and sayeth, "You have done a good work and you are, indeed, to be of good service to the Shining One in those times ahead. This, I knoweth of you."

Lom-Sa responds to him, "I am ever one with you. And whatsoever is to be done, I shall, as you are willing, do it with you."

Yo-El sayeth, "Then it is so, Lom-Sa."

We look upon one another with such awe and wonder, for we knoweth only, that which they are sharing to be of the nature as the Shining One has said ... that there shall be a time ahead, as they measure it in the Earth, when a great Call shall come.

We move close to them, those of us who have ever journeyed with Yo-El and Il-Em and the others, and we say to them, "We are ever with you, as well. That which has been done in our Father's Name to bring forth that of the Father's greatest gift we take within and we hold as a truth all throughout. We shall bear it for you in any works as you call upon us to serve you with. And in the spirit of you, Lom-Sa, we sayeth to these, our brethren, we too, are ever with you."

The Guardian cometh forth, to stand before us all. With his beautiful light, he gives unto us a blessing and unto those who have come from the No-Place Earth (in their new freewill-choice-freedom), who have come to join us and take up this same promise. The Guardian blesses them and we into oneness, saying to us, "What you pledge shall be a part of what is known as the Living Promise ... that wheresoever one calleth out unto the Father, there shall be that answer in His name. I, as the Guardian of the Way, shall ever be with you."

So, we turn to each of you
and we say to you only this:

This has been given because it has been asked.

It is given only that the Way may be illuminated and that you may choose, for within each of you is that as you have heard recounted here and greater. This we affirm.

Yet, it is to the honor of those who have gone before, and who stand with you in the present, that we celebrate this. It is retold again and again in the "heavens," that the Promise, ever, lives on, and that those who are one with it may journey and serve it in the joy and love of our Father.

His peace be with thee and His love be that which comforts you.

Dear Father,
I breathe in Your Peace.
I breathe It in,
living It,
and It becomes who I am.

I know Your Love to be without limit.
I know the Honor of oneness with You
to be beyond limitation.
I hold Your Truth within me,
knowing It to be Your spirit giving life to all that is.
With Your Compassion,
I meet that which comes to me,
allowing it to pass through me, unchanged,
as it wishes.
Whenever life turns to challenge me,
I give it Your eternal blessing ...
Your Grace.

I see Your Peace going before me in all that I am.
And
I
AM
FREE

ABOUT LAMA SING

More than thirty years ago for our convenience, the one through whom this information flows accepted the name Lama Sing, though it was stated they, themselves, have no need for names or titles.

"We identify ourselves only as servants of God, dedicated to you, our brothers and sisters in the Earth."
–Lama Sing

ಇ

ABOUT THIS CHANNEL

"Channel is that term given generally to those who enable themselves to be, as much as possible, open and passable in terms of information that can pass through them from the Universal Consciousness, or other such which are not associated in the direct sense with their finite consciousness of the current incarnation."
–Lama Sing

Books by Al Miner & Lama Sing ...

The Promise: *Book I of The Essene Legacy*
The Awakening: *Book II of The Essene Legacy*
The Path: *Book III of The Essene Legacy*

In Realms Beyond: *Book I of The Peter Chronicles*
In Realms Beyond Study Guide: *Questions and Answers*
Awakening Hope: *Book II of The Peter Chronicles*

Death, Dying, and Beyond: *How to Prepare for The Journey* Vol I
The Sea of Faces: *How to Prepare for The Journey* Vol II

Jesus: *Book I*
Jesus: *Book II*

The Course in Mastery

Watch for ...

Sacred City

The complete books of The Peter Chronicles

The complete books of The Peter Chronicles Study Guides:
    Companion Guides to the Peter Chronicles
    consisting of questions from study groups
    about the Peter Chronicles
    with answers from Lama Sing

The Movie/TV Series based on The Peter Project

For a comprehensive list of readings transcripts available, visit the
Lama Sing library at www.lamasing.net

ABOUT AL MINER

A chance hypnosis session in 1973 began Al's tenure as the channel for Lama Sing. Since then, nearly 10,000 readings have been given in a trance state answering technical and personal questions on such topics as science, health and disease, history, geophysical, spiritual, philosophical, metaphysical, past and future times, and much more. The validity of the information has been substantiated and documented by research institutions and individuals, and those receiving personal readings continue to refer others to Al's work based on the accuracy and integrity of the information in their readings. In 1984, St. Johns University awarded Al an honorary doctoral degree in parapsychology.

Al conducts a variety of field research projects, as well as occasional workshops and lectures. He is no longer accepting requests for personal readings, but, rather, is devoting his remaining time to works intended to be good for all. Much of his current research is dedicated to the concept that the best of all guidance is that which comes from within. Al lives with his family in the mountains of Western North Carolina.

7721377R0

Made in the USA
Lexington, KY
10 December 2010